Focus on the Sacraments

Peter Wilkinson

Kevin Mayhew Publishers

About the Author

Peter Wilkinson is a priest in the Archdiocese of Liverpool. He studied theology at universities in Rome and Manchester, and has been a member of the staffs of the Senior Seminaries at Upholland and Ushaw. Until his recent appointment as parish priest to St Clare's in Liverpool, he had served as a member of staff at the Upholland Northern Institute. He is Secretary of the Catholic Theological Association of Great Britain and Secretary of the Episcopal Theology Commission of England and Wales. His special area of concern is sacramental theology, and he recently pioneered a series of courses at Upholland on pastoral care of the dying.

Author's Acknowledgements

I would like to thank Sister Alice Simm for providing the inspiration for the symbolic presentation on the cover and for being a source of encouragement throughout the whole project; the Rev Christopher Fallon for his valuable help in the chapter on Marriage; and the staff of the Upholland Northern Institute, both past and present, from whom I have learnt so much in the work of Adult Christian Education.

Dedication

In memory of my mother.

All scripture texts are taken from *The Jerusalem Bible*, published and copyright 1966, 1967, and 1968 by Darton, Longman and Todd Ltd and Doubleday & Co Inc, and are used by permission of the publishers.

First published in Great Britain in 1987 by
KEVIN MAYHEW LTD.
Rattlesden, Bury St Edmunds, Suffolk IP30 0SZ

ISBN 0 86209 017 2

Cover and drawings of the seven symbols by Graham Scott
Other drawings by Deborah Meadows
Typesetting by Barry Sarling, Rayleigh, Essex
Printed by J.B. Offset (Marks Tey) Ltd., Colchester, Essex

CONTENTS

Introduction

At the heart of being a good Catholic is the experience of receiving the sacraments: children are to be baptised and later confirmed; we must attend Mass often and go to confession regularly in order to receive grace; the dying must be anointed. Because they represent the moment when we meet the Lord in a special way we have always been encouraged to receive them with devotion and understanding. In recent years, however, we have experienced a number of changes which some have welcomed as 'a breath of fresh air' and others have found disturbing and perplexing. Many welcome the use of English and the opportunity for more active participation while others regret the seeming loss of reverence, respect and, indeed, importance that was given to the sacraments in days gone by. If, then, the sacraments are to remain a central element of Christian people's lives, we need to understand some of the positive reasons underlying the need for change.

First of all, it was assumed that it was only in the sacraments that a real encounter with God became possible. Here in the sacraments, and in a way that doesn't happen elsewhere, one is near the Lord and united with him; one leaves behind the world of daily life. In this way, the sacraments appeared all too easily as religious rites which have nothing to do with real life in the world. Recent changes, therefore, have sought to emphasise that the sacraments are celebrations of the presence of Christ permeating every moment of our lives. Such familiar things as water, wine, oil and bread are intended to give us constant assurance that our God is with us. Today, more than ever, in a world which speaks so frequently of the absence of God, we need to be able to point at something within our grasp and say 'our God is here'.

Secondly, over the centuries, we have lost our sense of Christian fellowship. Our religion was very much a 'God and me' affair and, generally, we were quite oblivious to those around. Far from being a fellowship of loving believers, we were strangers to one another, not even knowing each others' names, much less their fears, their anxieties, and their longings. There was little sense of belonging to the Church to which each person made a contribution *(1 Corinthians 14:26)* according to his or her particular gift of the Spirit. Since childhood we have talked of going to Holy Communion, and yet, for so many of us, it has meant our own *individual* reception of the body and blood of Christ. And so, at the heart of recent changes has been the intention to transform our celebrations of the sacraments into community celebrations — opportunities for all of us to become actively involved.

Finally, there are two other areas which have been in need of renewal: the place of God's Word and the importance of symbolism. A most significant development has been the celebration of the sacraments in our own language. Now we are able to hear and understand God's invitation to come together for worship since all the sacraments are accompanied by a selection of readings from the Scriptures. The meaning of the sacraments is enriched too by the attention that is given to the symbolism of the sacraments. As we shall see, the basic elements of the sacraments — water, wine, oil and bread — are rich in meaning and unfold for us our true dignity as human beings and the quality of the created world in which we live. Through these simple means, God has adapted his way of loving to our human condition and enabled us to make some sense of the mystery which embraces us. Let us now examine the basic message which belongs to all the sacraments.

Our Need to sense God in a Broken World

A Century of Unparalleled Progress

We live in a complex and dangerous world with a history of poverty and death on a massive scale. This is particularly true of the twentieth century, so often characterised as one of unparalleled progress. In almost every area of human endeavour, whether it be in agriculture, in communication, in technology, in medicine, or in space exploration, there have been tremendous advances which have brought a large measure of abundance, comfort and health to the human community.

A Broken World of Suffering and Death

This same progress has been accompanied by suffering and death on a scale we can hardly imagine. Billions of pounds are spent year by year on weapons of war which can only kill and destroy, increasing the threat of nuclear holocaust. In a world in which the rich continually get richer, where vast human resources in terms of skill and ingenuity are used in making weapons of destruction, we hear of millions of people suffering from malnutrition in countries where one child in five dies at or shortly after birth. Television, especially through the remarkable initiative of Bob Geldof, has brought home to us in a dramatic way the terrible inequality of resources in our world: while we have mountains of grain going to waste in Europe, famine continues in Ethiopia, where the life expectancy is just 35 and many are unable to get medical help at all. The money required to provide adequate food, water, education, health and housing for everyone in the world, has been estimated at 12 billion pounds a year. It is a huge sum of money…about as much as the world spends on arms every two weeks!

We have our own Poor

In comparison to so many other countries throughout the world, Britain is a wealthy country. And yet, we know that we have our own poor as well: they are the powerless, the disadvantaged and the marginalised groups within our society. These include the poverty-stricken, victims of bad housing, the many thousands of young people with little prospect of work, and many groups of people with special needs: the elderly, the physically and mentally handicapped, and immigrant groups who are frequently subjected to various kinds of discrimination. These people have been hurt too much and too often and have little cause for rejoicing. They feel a sense of helplessness, trapped and imprisoned by their circumstances, enduring the pain of waiting without hope.

The World of God's Love

It is within such a world that we are called to celebrate the sacraments. Despite a natural feeling of helplessness in the face of so many issues, we take hold of water, bread, wine and oil — pieces of our broken world — and proclaim in faith that all that Jesus stood for endures for ever. Didn't Jesus promise a peace which this world cannot give and a joy that no one could take away? Did he not offer rest and refreshment to those who labour and are overburdened? Isn't the life he offers us frequently described in terms of being 'born again', 'regenerated and renewed', and 'changed into new creatures'? Didn't Jesus speak of rivers of living water, and the spring of water welling up into eternal life, water that will quench our thirst for ever? The message of the sacraments is that these are no empty promises. The love and mercy of God are final. The love of the Lord will never again be overcome. Such is the message

that is addressed to us every time we celebrate the sacraments of our Christian faith.

The Language of Sign and Symbol

Distinction between Signs and Symbols

We are familiar with the way *signs* play a part in communication: all drivers should abide by the signs contained in the highway code. They provide essential information and understanding, but, as signs, they are conventional and arbitrary. There is no built-in connection between the sign and what it seeks to convey.

Symbols, on the other hand, are rich in meaning. The word 'symbol' comes from the Greek word 'symballein' which means 'to bring together'. (Its opposite, 'diabolism', means to separate, to set in disarray.) Symbols, therefore, are by no means conventional and arbitrary; they touch our imaginations, emotions, desires and loves; they do not merely inform, they transform; they are able to express our most personal experiences. Examples of such symbols would be

the sense of touch;
the wedding ring;
water;
salt;
bread

— one could go on with a long list of symbols which speak to us on several levels of feeling and insight. But, for a variety of reasons, the world of symbols can seem alien to us.

A Loss of Symbolic Awareness

Within the Catholic tradition, when we speak of symbols, it is often assumed that we mean 'empty symbols'. How do we react, for example, when we say that the bread and wine are 'symbols' of the Lord's presence in the Eucharist? Centuries of polemical discussion have tended to separate the notion of 'symbol' from what is truly significant, from what is truly real. Little attention, therefore, has been given to the symbolism of the sacraments. It has been reduced to minimal proportions: a trickle of water for baptism; the traditional wafer for the Eucharist and communion under one kind; oil that is dabbed on only to be wiped off immediately (a far cry from the oil which pours down the beard of Aaron!); and, finally, little attention was given to the most powerful symbol of all, the gathering of people to celebrate the sacraments.

Furthermore, attitudes within our society have also dimmed our symbolic awareness. We tend to see reality primarily in terms of what can be measured and assessed. We are accustomed to classifying things and detailing their characteristics. We equate what is real with what is tangible and immediately within our grasp. Such is the persistent message of television: good looks, plenty of money, social status and professional success, are the only values. We miss so much of what lies beneath the surface. In the words of D.H. Lawrence:

> '...we are bleeding at the roots, because we are cut off from the earth and sun and stars.'
> (A propos of *Lady Chatterley's Lover*)

Recovery of Symbolism

A variety of developments in recent years has helped us to recover the symbolic nature of life and the world in which we live:

• we are indebted to the important studies of C. Jung in the field of depth psychology who has awakened us to the basic human symbols common to people of all time — what Jung calls archetypal symbols, the most important being water, fire and air;

• we have benefitted, too, from renewed appreciation of the Scriptures: they give shape to our common spiritual culture; they are the record of our history and provide us with the basic symbols that we share together like common property (water, light, bread, wine, oil and wind); they provide what we need for a common consciousness;

• and, finally, there is an increasing recognition, today, of the mysterious nature of physical reality. The further one examines it, whether at the level of outer space or at the atomic level, the more complex that reality shows itself to be. It is no surprise, therefore, that Teilhard de Chardin, as a scientist, cannot help but see that physical reality is charged through with mystery.

We are beginning to realise that the only way we can communicate, share ourselves, our stories and our innermost feelings, is by means of symbols.

The Power of Symbols

The most basic symbol at the heart of human communication must surely be the sense of touch. Hence the child's first experience of reality is the touch, the gesture of the mother; they are the most powerful ways in which she communicates her life and love. Throughout life, it is the human sense of touch that does so much to ease the pain of the heart, to dispel fear, and to communicate light, love and liberation.

©John Taylor

This experience of the power of symbols at the heart of human communication inevitably points to the fundamental symbolic nature of the world in which we live. In the words of the Psalmist: 'The heavens and the earth proclaim the glory of God' *(cf. Psalm 19:1)*, words echoed in John Newman's sermon *The Invisible World* given in 1837:

> 'Let these be your thoughts, my brethren, especially in the spring season, when the whole face of nature is so rich and beautiful. Once only in the year, yet once, does the world which we see show forth its hidden powers, and in a manner manifest itself. Then the leaves come out, and blossoms on the fruit trees and flowers; and the grass and corn spring up. There is a sudden rush and burst outwardly of that hidden life which God has lodged in the material world.'

Of all the prophets who have proclaimed the symbolic power of the world in which we live, St Francis of Assisi must be the most well-known. Towards the end of his life, when blind and in great pain, he wrote one of the greatest of all Christian hymns, the *Canticle of the Sun*. The created world and everything within it constantly reminded St Francis of the grandeur and the wonder of God himself: the rocks reminded him of that 'rock which was Christ'; the lambs of the field symbolised the Lamb of God, trees were symbols of the cross, and lights represented the Light of the World. Everything in the natural order led Francis' mind and heart to God.

Nearer to our own time, these same insights have found expression in Teilhard de Chardin's *Hymn of the Universe*:

'I had then the impression, as I gazed at the host, that its surface was gradually spreading out like a spot of oil but of course much more swiftly and luminously...through the mysterious expansion of the host, the whole world had become incandescent, had itself become like a giant host...the whiteness was consuming all things from within themselves. It had penetrated through the channels of matter into the inmost depths of all hearts...the immense host, having given life to everything, was now slowly contracting; and the treasures it was drawing into itself were joyously pressed close together with its living light.'

And finally, there is the vision of creation expressed so well over a hundred years ago by a Red Indian Chief speaking about the loss of his land to the white man:

'Every part of this earth is sacred to my people. Every shining pine needle, every sandy shore, every mist in the dark woods, every clearing and humming insect is holy in the memory and experience of my people. The sap which courses through the trees carries the memories of the red man.'

(Chief Seattle's Testimony)

It is only within such a sacramental view of the world that we are able to appreciate the sacraments of Christian faith. By making use of the simple things of this earth — water, bread, wine and oil, — we are enabled to see with fresh eyes the full richness of our dignity as human beings and the created world in which we live. We are reminded of the value and importance of everything that we are and do, especially in those most basic areas of human life: birth, marriage, human relationships and death. In our celebration of the sacraments, we know that every moment of our lives is charged with the grandeur of God. But it is to Christ that we must now turn; he is the fundamental sacrament (symbol) of the presence of God in our world; he is the source of our sacramental vision.

Jesus: the Sacrament of God's Presence

Jesus was born a Jew

In Jesus, we are able to know God in human terms; that is what it means when we say that Jesus is the sacrament of God's presence. Jesus makes God known to us by being man, by being one with us in flesh and blood. In particular, he was born of the Jewish people. What he taught, how he looked at the world, his relationship to God as Father, are all set in the context of the Judaism of his age.

At Home in our World

Because Jesus was our brother according to the flesh and felt so much at home in our world, he had an intimate appreciation of the beauty of creation, recognising everywhere the finger of his Father in heaven. His vision and imagination are expressed with such warmth and spontaneity in that most famous and lyrical of all passages in the Gospel — the sermon on the birds of the air and the lilies of the field *(Matthew 6:25-34)*. It is a picture trembling with life:

'Look at the birds in the sky. They do not sow or reap...Think of the flowers growing in the fields; they never have to work or spin...'

Jesus wants us to wear the smile of those flowers, have the carefree attitude of the birds, so that all may come to associate godliness with life and freedom. He wants to enlarge our awareness, to make us see reality through his kind and penetrating eyes.

On another occasion, Jesus pictures God as the poor woman who scrambles after the coin that rolls away on the mud floor in her dark little house, for God is most anxious to rescue any bit of his precious creation that may be rolling away from him. In so many ways, Jesus speaks of that compassionate providence of God which is so intimately involved in keeping the world which he created secure in his love.

Jesus is the Compassion of God

What Jesus confirms above all, though, is the passionate devotion of God for his people — a love which is utterly inexhaustible and extravagant, constantly assuring them of healing, forgiveness and newness of life. It is easy to understand why the sense of touch was so important in the life of Jesus. Children are brought to Jesus 'for him to touch them' *(Luke 18:15)*; he heals the crippled woman *(Luke 13:13)* and the daughter of Jairus *(Luke 8:54)* by laying his hands on them; the woman with a haemorrhage is cured by reaching out and touching the hem of Jesus' garment *(Luke 8:44)*; and a frequent experience of Jesus was 'that everyone in the crowd was trying to touch him because power came out of him that cured them all' *(Luke 6:19)*. These people received nothing but kindness and compassion; he encouraged them out of their paralysis, he released them from their crippling physical and psychological burdens, he brought them back to life.

What explains the impact of Jesus is nothing less than his sheer humanity; he presents himself as one who understands the weakness of the human condition from personal experience. A most dramatic scriptural text in this respect comes from the Letter to the Hebrews:

> 'For it is not as if we had a high priest who was incapable of feeling our weaknesses with us; but we have one who has been tempted in every way that we are, though he is without sin...he can sympathise with those who are ignorant or uncertain because he too lives in the limitations of weakness...'
>
> *Hebrews 4:15-16; 5:1*

Because of his experience of human weakness, Jesus is able to reach out to every kind of human suffering. He gradually enters into those domains of injustice, oppression and evil, in which the compassion of God is most needed. In his moment of darkness, naked and crucified upon the cross, Jesus embraces all men and women, sharing with them that sense of abandonment, the terrible fear that their lives are without meaning. He enters into their situation of suffering all the way to the bitter end and, in the words of Teresa of Avila, becomes an ever present and most extraordinary companion and friend.

Jesus is 'the Image of the Unseen God'

As we reflect on the human experience of Jesus, we affirm in faith that in Jesus we have to do with nothing less than God himself. There lies the uniqueness of the human life of Jesus: it speaks in language that we can understand of a heart shaped by immeasurable love — the inner heart of God passionately concerned for his people. Here lies the starting-point for all Christian understanding of the sacraments: the person of Jesus in the flesh is the sacrament of God's presence amongst his people. In the words of St Paul's letter to the Colossians: 'He is the image of the unseen God' *(Colossians 1:15-16)*. And in St John's Gospel: 'He who has seen me has seen the Father' *(John 14:9)*.

This same God who made his name known to us in the person of Jesus Christ nearly two thousand years ago is active in our lives today within the Church. It is now through the flesh and blood of people whose

BBC Hulton Picture Library

lives are shaped by the life of the risen Lord that our God proclaims his presence to a broken world. In the words of St Teresa of Avila:

> 'Christ has now no body on earth but yours; no hands but yours; no feet but yours; yours are the eyes through which Christ looks out with compassion to the world; yours are the feet through which he is to go about doing good; yours are the hands through which he is to bless people today.'

We need to look a little more closely at an understanding of the Church as the sacrament of Christ's presence in the world.

The Church as the Sacrament of Christ's Presence

We are the Body of Christ

In the moment of Christ's death, the Church was born. From earliest times this has been the meaning given to St John's reference concerning the blood and water coming from the side of Christ:

> 'When they came to Jesus, they found he was already dead, and so instead of breaking his legs one of the soldiers pierced his side with a lance and immediately there came out blood and water.'
>
> (John 19:33)

Blood and water, of course, are understood to refer to the two principal sacraments of the Church, baptism and Eucharist. For St Paul, too, we are so inseparable from the resurrection itself, that he can only speak of us as the body of Christ. This lay at the heart of his Damascus experience: 'Saul, Saul, why are you persecuting me?' *(Acts 9:4)*. And again:

> 'I have been crucified with Christ, and I live now not with my own life but with the life of Christ who lives in me.'
>
> (Galatians 2:20)

It is appropriate that St Paul should speak of us as the 'body of Christ'. From personal experience, we know that we can only make ourselves present to one another, share ourselves, our stories, our innermost feelings, by means of our bodies. We cannot see inside another person directly; we can only grasp their spirit, the power that drives them on, through the rich vocabulary of word and gesture which finds expression by means of our bodies. It is through our bodies that we become one with our family and friends, our towns and cities, indeed, with the whole of creation. In a similar way, says St Paul, the Christian community is called to live as the 'body' of the risen Christ — to make visible by means of our own flesh and blood, the presence of the risen Christ in space and time.

Sense of Belonging

In practical terms, being the body of Christ means that Jesus calls us to create a real sense of belonging within the Church and within our parish communities: for newcomers, for young people, single people, single parent families, the divorced and remarried, the unemployed, the sick, the handicapped, the house-bound and the elderly — indeed, all those whom Jesus calls his own. Being in communion with one another in Jesus Christ means a new way of living together which says that no one is alone with his or her disabilities; we are all, without exception, called to be part of the one body of Christ.

At the Service of Others

If we are truly the body of Christ, giving shape to the quality of love that comes from the heart of Christ, we should constantly touch the lives of the hungry of the world with generous compassion and understanding; we should draw on the bread of life that is Jesus so that we ourselves might become the bread of life for those in need. In the midst of a world in which there is so much poverty, suffering and death, we must constantly be a sign of hope in the risen Christ, not afraid to face up to the challenge of the Gospel. Through us those words of Jesus should sound loud and clear:

> **'Come to me all you who labour and are overburdened, and I will give you rest. Shoulder my yoke and learn from me, for I am gentle and humble in heart. Yes, my yoke is easy and my burden light.'**
>
> *Matthew 11:28ff*

The Church as Sacrament

Because we who belong to the Church are the body of Christ, the Church itself can be called a 'sacrament' and is therefore described by Vatican II in the following terms:

> *'By virtue of its relation to Christ, the Church is a kind of sacrament of intimate communion with God and of the unity of all mankind, that is, she is a sign and instrument of such union and unity.'*
> (Lumen Gentium, no. 1)

This means that the Church of its very nature is sacramental and all its activities, no matter how seemingly insignificant, are sacramental too:

> *'[Jesus] happened to notice a poverty-stricken widow putting in two small coins, and he said, "I tell you truly, this poor widow has put in more than any of them..."'*
> (Luke 21:3)

What we term the seven sacraments, however, are most expressive of the Church's inner life. And so, for example, we are able to experience the forgiveness of Jesus in many ways in the life of the Church: through the experience of friendship and understanding, through prayer and reading the Scriptures. But, in the sacrament of forgiveness and reconciliation, we come to know in a special way the forgiving heart of Jesus which touches the deepest areas of alienation in our lives. We are led to identify and repent of our sins, we know that we are truly forgiven, and we are enabled to change our lives. In this sacrament, we experience in a special way the Church as the sacrament of the forgiveness of Christ. The same can be said of the other sacraments as they bring into focus different aspects of the essential nature of the Church as the sacrament of the risen Christ in our midst.

Why Seven Sacraments?

Many reasons have been given as to why there should be *seven* sacraments. St Thomas Aquinas draws on the analogy of the various stages of human life: birth, maturity, alienation, human love, vocation, sickness and death. The seven sacraments, therefore, symbolise the action of Jesus taking hold of the most basic areas of human life and filling them with his love. Further-more, he pointed out that it was fitting that there should be seven sacraments because seven is a number which symbolises wholeness, the sevenfold gift of the Spirit, the creative love of God penetrating to the depths of human life wherever it is to be found.

Let us now look at each one of the sacraments in turn, reflecting on their historical development, their essential meaning within the Christian faith, and their celebration in the life of the Church today.

Further Reading

Cooke, Bernard. *Sacraments and Sacramentality*, Twenty-Third Publs., 1983

Crichton, J.D. *Christian Celebration*, Chapman, 1981

Feider, Paul A. *The Sacraments: encountering the risen Lord*, Ave Maria Press, 1986

Fourez, Gerard. *Sacraments and Passages*, Ave Maria Press, 1983

Grey, Mary C. *In Search of the Sacred*, Anthony Clarke, 1983

Guzie, Tad. *The Book of Sacramental Basics*, Paulist Press, 1981

Hellwig, Monika K. *The Meaning of the Sacra-ments*, Pflaum Press, 1972

Lavery, Hugh. *Sacraments*, Darton, Longman & Todd, 1980

Martos, Joseph. *Doors to the Sacred*, SCM Press, 1981

The Pope in Britain, St Paul Publications, 1982

Purnell, Patrick. *Our Faith Story*, Collins, 1985

Roberts, William P. *Encounters with Christ*, Paulist Press, 1985

BAPTISM

Introduction: Why Baptism?

We are familiar with many traditional reasons given for having a child baptised; Nigel Bavidge lists the following in his popular series on the Sacraments:

- ▲ he will have bad luck if he's not baptised;

- ▲ she will miss out on a lot of presents if she's not 'done' properly;

- ▲ your mother would like him to be baptised;

- ▲ if she's baptised she can go to the Catholic school down the road.

A more fundamental reason, however, would be that a child must be baptised as soon as possible after birth in order to be freed from original sin and so given access to the life of God. Tremendous anxiety surrounded the possibility of a child dying without being baptised. The Church as a whole did not accept St Augustine's theory that unbaptised babies would go to hell, even though only in a mild form! A commonly accepted answer was that unbaptised children went to a place of purely natural happiness called 'Limbo'. This was increasingly found to be most unsatisfactory in the face of parents' basic instinct that such children could only possibly be with the Lord.

But more basic questions are being asked these days. More and more parents are reluctant to have their children baptised. They want to know what possible meaning baptism could have at such an age and ask whether it would not be much more appropriate to delay baptism until such time that the individual can decide for himself or herself. The Church, they say, requires a deep commitment from all those who are baptised and, surely, this can only come from a free choice. Such are just some of the questions we need to bear in mind as we reflect upon the richness of the Church's tradition concerning this fundamental sacrament.

The Scriptural Origins of Baptism

Background to Christian Baptism

■ Proselyte Baptism

The roots of Christian baptism lie within Judaism. Our attention might first be drawn towards the many purification rituals which characterise the Jewish religion and to which Jesus refers on a number of occasions (Mark 7:1-5). In addition to these, later Judaism knew a form of water rite known as proselyte baptism, whereby gentiles were received into Judaism. It consisted of three phases: instruction in the Law, circumcision for males, and a water bath for all involving considerable amounts of water, and not just a trickle!

■ Old Testament Covenant

But the basic roots of baptism are to be found in the Old Testament concept of covenant, whereby God takes the initiative in reaching out to his people and inviting them to make a response in faith. The sign of God's covenant with Abraham was circumcision and this became the distinctive mark of belonging to the Jewish people, the chosen ones of God. In view of our later discussion on infant baptism, it is interesting to note at this point that it was taken for granted that one could enter into a special relationship with God at the beginning of one's life.

■ The Baptism of John

The Gospels themselves, however, point to the real prototype of Christian baptism: the baptism of John. This dramatic figure proclaimed a forceful message concerning the imminence of the kingdom of God:

> **'Repent, for the kingdom of God is close at hand.'**
>
> *Matthew 3:2*

His baptism is a call to repentance and, unlike other washing rites of late Judaism, John's baptism is not self-administered. Furthermore, as an indication of the

extreme urgency of his message, his baptism was not repeatable but could only be received once. Nevertheless, John's baptism was not the final word. He distinguishes between his own baptism, and that of the one who is to come. He contrasts his own baptism with a future baptism in the Holy Spirit *(Mark 1:8)*.

Baptism of Jesus

Jesus himself was baptised by John *(Mark 1:9-11)*. In this way, he not only showed that he fully shared in the human condition but also that he approved of John's baptism and his call to repentance *(Mark 1:4)*. It marks a unique moment in the experience of Jesus when, empowered by the Spirit, he embarks upon his public ministry which will ultimately bring him to his death on the cross.

Indeed, the real baptism of Jesus is his death. And so we read in *Luke 12:50*:

> *'There is a baptism I must still receive, and how great is my distress till it is over!'*

And again in *Mark 10:38*:

> *' "You do not know what you are asking", Jesus said to them. "Can you drink the cup that I must drink, or be baptised with the baptism with which I must be baptised?" '*

These texts bring home to us the close relationship between the sacrament of baptism and the event of the cross by which Jesus saved us. It is then, above all, that we are able to recognise the full extent of God's love for each of us. The message of the cross says simply: 'the name of God is "God-with-us" and he will enable us to overcome every situation which seems to threaten us'. Such is the real significance of the baptism of Jesus.

'Baptise all nations...'

It is evident that the early Church began to baptise very shortly after Easter. In the spring of 54, St Paul wrote to the community at Corinth:

> *'In the one Spirit we were all baptised, Jews as well as Greeks, slaves as well as citizens, and one Spirit was given to us all to drink.'*
>
> (1 Corinthians 12:13)

And again, writing to the Romans in 56 or 57:

> *'You have been taught that when we were baptised in Christ Jesus we were baptised in his death.'*
>
> (Romans 6:3)

After the stunning experience of Pentecost, when they were filled with the Holy Spirit *(Acts 2:2-4)*, they were ready to proclaim with boldness the saving message of Jesus. They themselves had not been immersed in water for baptism, but remembering the example of Jesus, they saw the value of using water to enable people to feel washed clean of the past and refreshed and renewed in the Spirit of the risen Christ.

During this period, the basic rite of baptism consisted of the following elements:

- proclamation of the Gospel always preceded baptism;
- it marked a real moment of conversion;
- such conversion was followed by baptism by immersion;
- it was followed by quite a change of lifestyle.

> *'These remained faithful to the teaching of the apostles, to the brotherhood, to the breaking of bread and to prayers.'*
>
> (Acts 2:42)

Most converts to the Christian way would inevitably be adults, but it is more than likely that the children were baptised as well. In the Acts of the Apostles we read that Lydia *and her whole household* were baptised after Paul and Timothy had preached in Philippi *(Acts 16:11-15)*. On another occasion, a jailer was baptised with all his family *(Acts 16:25-33)*. Presumably such families would have included some children. Furthermore, it seems inconceivable that children would have been prohibited in view of the words of Jesus:

> 'I tell you solemnly, unless you change and become like little children you will never enter the kingdom of heaven. And so, the one who makes himself as little as this little child is the greatest in the kingdom of heaven.'
>
> *Matthew 18:3*

Developing Patterns of Christian Initiation

The Age of the Catechumenate

One of the earliest detailed descriptions of Christian initiation is to be found in a document entitled: *The Apostolic Tradition of Hippolytus*, a Roman liturgy of the early third century:

'Let a catechumen be instructed for three years. But if a man be earnest and persevere well in the matter, let him be received, because it is not the time that is judged but the conduct.'

'And when they are chosen who are set apart to receive baptism let their life be examined, whether they live piously while catechumens, whether they "honoured the widows", whether they visited the sick, whether they have fulfilled every good work.'

'When they come to the water, let the water be pure and flowing. And they shall put off their clothes. And they shall baptise the little children first. And if they can answer for themselves, let them answer. But if they cannot, let their parents answer or someone from their family.'

Candidates wishing to enter the Christian community were called **Catechumens** and their period of preparation could last for as long as three years. During this time they would be sponsored by a member of the community and given instruction on the kind of behaviour expected of Christians. Instruction on the mysteries of the faith would first be given during the intensive period of preparation just prior to their baptism. Initially, this would take place just once a year, normally during the celebration of Easter or some other special feast like Pentecost. After the threefold immersion or pouring of water, Christians were clothed in white garments, anointed by the bishop, and finally admitted to the table of the Eucharist. During this time, the rite was obviously intended primarily for adults but, as we have already noted, from earliest times infants and older children were also regarded as suitable candidates for full Christian initiation.

Breakdown of this Pattern

As early as the fourth century, this pattern of Christian initiation began to break down. After 313, when the Christian religion became officially recognised, the number of baptisms increased dramatically. The bishops could not keep up with such a rapid growth of the Church and so they would later visit the local churches to confirm the baptisms carried out the previous Easter or Pentecost. This second anointing by the bishop gradually became the sacrament of confirmation. By the end of the fifth century, infant baptism became the norm and this inevitably brought about fundamental changes in the rite itself and provoked new theological questions.

■ Changes in the Rite

Because of the necessity of baptism, parents were encouraged to have their children baptised as soon as possible after birth and not to wait for the annual baptism at Easter. Indeed, they were soon allowed to be baptised at any time of the year, so that by the fourteenth century *the baptismal ceremony disappeared from the Easter Vigil altogether*. In the process, it increasingly became a private ceremony witnessed only by the godparents and the immediate family.

Once infant baptism became the norm, and people ceased to look upon the Christian commitment as something radical, calling for an explicit choice, the time for preparation was no longer felt to be necessary. Since everyone was regarded as a Christian, within Europe at least, baptism was looked upon as part of the ordinary pattern of life which people received without much choice or reflection. Furthermore, *the rites surrounding baptism were gradually reduced to a minimum*: the general practice of immersion changed into the familiar ritual of pouring with the baptismal formula being pronounced by the priest or minister: 'I baptise you in the name of the Father...'; the exorcisms and anointings are retained; but now the sponsors responded on behalf of the children being baptised. What had once been a marvellous liturgy, celebrated over a number of years, had now become telescoped into a ritual act performed all on the one occasion.

■ New Theological Questions

The practice of infant baptism inevitably gave rise to the question: *why baptise babies?* St Augustine was to provide an answer which would have a profound effect upon Catholic consciousness down to the present day. Drawing heavily on St Cyprian's earlier teaching that all are born with the sin of Adam on their soul, he developed it further. Briefly, he taught that because of original sin we are all involved in personal guilt from the moment of conception:

'For what reason therefore should he (the godparent) say that he (the child) renounced the devil, if there was nothing of the devil in him? that he should be turned towards God, if he was

not turned away from him? that he believed in the remission of sins...when none could be attributed to him?'

(cf. E.C. Whitaker, *Documents of the Baptismal Liturgy*)

> **'Let the little children alone, and do not stop them coming to me; for it is to such as these that the kingdom of heaven belongs.'**
>
> *Matthew 19:14*

In other words, St Augustine argues, there would be no need for exorcism when baptising children. They need to be forgiven.

This brings us to the question: *what do we mean by original sin?* St Augustine describes its meaning in the strongest terms:

'From the time when our nature sinned in paradise...we have all become one lump of clay, a lump of sin. Since then, by sinning, we have forfeited our merit and God's mercy is withdrawn from us so that we sinners are owed nothing but eternal damnation.'

(cf. E. Yarnold, *The Theology of Original Sin*)

These words represent a fundamental truth of the Gospel: everyone, without exception, is radically dependent on Jesus Christ: 'for cut off from me you can do nothing' *(John 15:5)*. Such is the essential meaning of the teaching of the Church on original sin. But St Augustine goes too far in suggesting that we are all involved in personal guilt from the moment of conception. Rather, when we are conceived we become one with the radical sinfulness of the human race and will inevitably sin unless we have access to the life that comes to us from the heart of Christ.

What happens, then, to children who die before baptism? St Augustine would have to say they would be damned, although their punishment would be mild. For this reason, he argued, every child had to be baptised immediately after birth lest they die and go to hell. The Church as a whole did not accept St Augustine's theory but it did not know exactly where children went after death. A popular tradition grew up whereby unbaptised babies were sent to a place called **Limbo** — a state of natural happiness which excluded the possibility of heaven. The Church has neither denied nor affirmed the existence of such a place.

The word 'limbo' means 'margin' or 'periphery' and, apparently, the original answer of theologians was: 'We will have to place the question concerning the destiny of unbaptised babies *in the margin* because we simply do not know'. By some confusion, it became a special place for unbaptised children on the other side of death (a point of view attributed to Monika Hellwig, cf. M. & D. Linn/S. Fabricant, *Healing the Greatest Hurt*, pp.108 ff.).

The traditional teaching has been simple enough: 'We do not know. But we do know that God is merciful'. Today, we are able to speak with much more confidence of the destiny of love that awaits such children in view of all that we know of our God who says in Jesus Christ:

Such confidence, however, must not obscure the terrible pain that so often accompanies it. Parents who lose a baby experience just as much grief as they would following the death of any loved person and need all the community support and encouragement necessary to express such grief. (cf. M. & D. Linn/S. Fabricant, *Healing the Greatest Hurt*, pp.108-139).

St Augustine

BBC Hulton Picture Library

The Road to Recovery

The Church's traditional practice of baptising infants is undoubtedly soundly based. From the beginning, parents have intuitively sensed that it was right to bring them into the community of Christians soon after they were born and make them welcome there. The children's readiness and desire are held in trust for a while by their parents whose own faith is strong and whose way of life gives clear promise that their children will develop in the faith of the Church.

Unfortunately, through lack of adequate preparation and continuing Christian education, such faith has been lacking. Children have often been baptised indiscriminately and this, over the years, has given rise to a multitude of Christians who are so only in name. It is for this reason that renewal is underway with the gradual introduction of the *Rite of Christian Initiation of Adults*. It emphasises the radical commitment involved in the sacrament of baptism and seeks to recover the richness of Christian tradition as expressed, for example, in *The Apostolic Tradition of Hippolytus*, quoted earlier. We will first examine the various stages involved in this new rite before reflecting on the tremendous challenge it presents to the Church in our own time.

The Rite of Christian Initiation of Adults

The Rite of Christian Initiation of Adults (from now on referred to as RCIA) was first published in 1972 and is now becoming well known in the experience of many of our parishes. It describes a process by which the Church is to receive would-be converts into the Church. Such people are once again referred to as *Catechumens*, meaning 'ones being instructed' or 'learners', and their preparation is known as the catechumenate. The whole process is divided into various stages and each stage is marked by a special rite of its own.

The Stage of Inquiry (The Pre-Catechumenate)

The first of these stages is that of inquiry and can take place quite informally, within a family, at work, at a meeting, when serious interest in the Gospel and the life of the Church begins to make its presence felt. It is a time
— for people to hear the Gospel of Jesus Christ in such a way that they are able to say yes or no;
— for listening and sharing our stories of faith and search for meaning;
— of welcome and hospitality, reflecting the warmth of the love that comes from the heart of God.

Throughout this time, which must take as long as is necessary, the possibility of choice must be left wide open.

Becoming a Catechumen

■ The Rite of Entry

This is the moment of commitment and is marked with a special form of celebration: the rite of entry. It takes place in the presence of the congregation and welcomes the enquirers, along with their sponsors who will continue to help them in their journey of faith. The priest calls the candidates by name and asks them what they are looking for. After they have declared their rejection of evil and their desire for faith, the celebrant then admits them as catechumens and signs them with a cross. They are then members of the Church; although not yet baptised, they belong to the community. The early Fathers of the Church spoke of becoming a catechumen as a type of conception, in which the catechumen is implanted into the womb of the Church. Baptism is, then, a new birth which takes place only after a necessary period of formation. After the liturgy of the Word, the celebrant dismisses the candidates, recalling the joy with which the catechumens were received, and exhorting them to live according to the Word they have received.

■ Being a Catechumen

The pastoral formation of the catechumens 'continues until they have matured sufficiently in their conversion of faith. If necessary, it may last for several years.' (RCIA, 98). It depends on where people are when they start; we are all on a journey to God and not everyone is at the same point in the journey. We have

Last night of a series of training sessions to form a Welcoming Community to begin RCIA; Sacred Heart Church, Wimbledon. November 1986.

© Mary Brennan

experienced different stories of faith; we have received varied kinds of support and encouragement. All of this needs to be taken into account during this time when the main work of learning to know Christ takes place. Catechumens are helped to an awareness of God and his love, to a personal knowledge of Jesus and his teaching, and to an experience of what it means to belong to the Church.

Growth in faith during this time is sustained by three kinds of liturgical rites:

— celebrations of the liturgy of the Word, to encourage a life of faith ever attentive to the Word of God; these may constitute the first part of Mass to enable catechumens to become familiar with the pattern of worship within the community; in this case, the dismissal after the liturgy of the Word must be done in a sensitive way that doesn't cause difficulty or misunderstanding;

— blessings and exorcisms, prayers which ask for the courage, joy and peace that are needed in the struggle to live the Christian life;

— rites of passage, which normally take the form of an anointing with oil, symbolising the power and strength which God gives the catechumens to sustain them in their conversion; the oil of catechumens now comes into its own.

Special emphasis is given to the part the community plays:

> *'This Christian initiation, which takes place during the catechumenate, should not be left entirely to the priests and catechists, but should be the concern of the whole Christian community, especially of the sponsors, so that from the beginning the catechumens will feel that they belong to the People of God.'*
>
> (Decree on Missionary Activity, para. 14)

The whole community has a responsibility for welcoming catechumens not only into their local parish but also into their homes, to share with them their experience of faith, and to support them with their presence and prayers. Particular importance is given to sponsors whose task is to accompany catechumens as friends on their journey of faith, and to speak up on their behalf at the various stages of initiation.

The Period of Purification and Enlightenment

■ The Rite of Election

On the first Sunday of Lent the rite of election is celebrated when the catechumens ask to receive the sacraments of initiation during the Easter Vigil. The rite marks the end of the catechumenate and the beginning of a deeper, more intense form of preparation during the season of Lent. They are called forward by name, together with their sponsors and godparents, who testify to their readiness for baptism. The celebrant then invites the candidates to go forward towards the sacraments of initiation and to write their names in a special register.

■ Scrutinies and Presentations

During the period of preparation throughout Lent, the Church calls for the celebration of the scrutinies and the presentations. The purpose of the scrutinies is clearly stated by the new rite:

> *'The scrutinies are intended to purify the catechumens' minds and hearts, to strengthen them against temptation, to purify their intentions, and to make firm their decision, so that they remain more closely united with Christ and make progress in their efforts to love God more deeply.'*
>
> (RCIA 154)

© Mary Brennan

Baptism, Confirmation (Adults), Eucharist, at St Thomas More, Manor House, 1987.

©*Mary Brennan*

Baptism at St Thomas More, Manor House, Easter Vigil, 1987.

These scrutinies are celebrated in the presence of the community on the third, fourth, and fifth Sundays of Lent, during Mass, when the Gospel readings speak of the Samaritan woman, the man born blind, and the raising of Lazarus. In this way, the elect come to know Jesus as the source of living water, the light of the world, and our resurrection and life. The presentations are short ceremonies during which the elect are presented with the Creed and the Lord's Prayer, representing the summary of the Church's faith and prayer.

■ Celebration of the Sacraments of Initiation

During the Easter Vigil, the elect celebrate the three sacraments of initiation: Baptism, Confirmation and Eucharist. In the words of the RCIA:

> *'They are admitted into the people of God, receive the adoption of the sons of God, and are led by the Holy Spirit into the promised fullness of time, and in the Eucharistic sacrifice and meal, to the banquet of the kingdom of God.'*
>
> (no.27)

After the renunciation of Satan and the profession of faith, those to be baptised are 'plunged into the waters' to symbolise their sharing in the death and resurrection of Jesus and being made one with the People of God. Oil, a lighted candle, and a white garment are all used to signify the life in Christ of the newly baptised. But the principal symbol is *water*. In human experience, water is life-giving: it enables plants to grow, it quenches our thirst, it cleanses and purifies; but water, too, can wreak havoc and inflict sudden death. It is not surprising, therefore, that water should be such a powerful symbol in the Scriptures of the blessings and the richness of life that comes from God, especially in the person of Jesus Christ:

> **'Anyone who drinks the water that I shall give will never be thirsty again: the water that I shall give will turn into a spring inside him, welling up to eternal life.'**
>
> *John 4:14*

All of this comes to a focal point in the waters of baptism. Immediately following baptism, the celebrant confers the sacrament of confirmation, which is then followed by the celebration of the Eucharist, the 'climax of their initiation'.

The Period of Mystagogia

This period extends throughout the fifty days of the Easter season and emphasises that the rites of initiation are not an end, but a new beginning. Together with their godparents and the community of the faithful, the newly baptised are encouraged to reflect on all that has happened to them and to recognise that their journey in faith is a lifelong process. In the words of the RCIA:

> *'The time of postbaptismal catechesis is of great importance so that the neophytes, helped by their sponsors, may enter into a closer relationship with the faithful and bring them renewed vision and a new impetus.'*
>
> (no.39)

Such a process of initiation inevitably represents a tremendous challenge to the whole Church. It is a call to continuous conversion because we cannot demand more of the newly baptised than is expected of all the baptised within the Church. We need to listen carefully to the kind of Church we are called to be.

© Carlos Reyes

What Kind of Church Baptises?

A Church of Hospitality and Friendship

People will only make enquiries about our way of life within the Church if they are attracted by what they see; they will only persevere in their process of conversion if they are continually supported by acceptance and friendship. As a Christian community, therefore, we are called first and foremost to be a place of welcome where we are able to breathe and recognise that God is our Father whose love embraces us in every moment of the day. Such need for welcome and friendship arises against a background of fears and anxieties. We live in a broken world in which there is so much suffering, so much darkness and so many trials. We are right to be apprehensive. Within the Church, in the Spirit of Christ, we are called to face up to the tensions that inevitably come our way and proclaim our faith in the God who will always keep us safe in his hands.

Called to share in the Death and Resurrection of Jesus

Through baptism, we are drawn into communion with a God who is passionately concerned for the liberation of his people. This urgency of the will of God is dramatically expressed in the person of Jesus Christ who came to save that which was lost. We recognise, in the death of Jesus especially, the response of God to the deepest hunger of the human heart. As his people, we believe that Jesus' new life has broken the universal rule of death; his freedom has prevailed, his way has led to life, his Spirit is truly at work in our world.

'We are the Body of Christ'

Through the whole process of Christian initiation, and especially in the moment of baptism itself, we are called by name whereby we recognise that every living person without exception has a unique dignity which is genuinely worthy of eternal life. Before God, no one is anonymous; every man, woman and child counts; not a hair falls from our heads without our heavenly Father noticing. And yet, no one can say to another 'I have no need of you'. We need sponsors, friends, the whole Christian community. We belong together in the body of Christ *(1 Corinthians 12:26)*. Being in communion means a new way of belonging together; we are called upon to breathe new life into one another, to create an experience of friendship with one another, to draw out from one another what is best in each. No one must feel alone or isolated within the body of Christ. God is *our* Father.

Baptism creates a Sacramental Bond of Unity

In baptism, we make our own the prayer of Jesus:

> **'May they all be one. Father, may they be one in us,**
>
> **as you are in me and I am in you.'**
>
> *John 17:21*

In practice, this means making friends with members of other Churches, acknowledging them as our brothers and sisters in Jesus Christ; setting aside all forms of caricature and rash judgement, respecting their love for Christ and their dedication to the Gospel; and praying not just *for* one another but *with* one another, experiencing the tremendous depth of communion we share together in the one Lord and in the one Spirit. It is only through the love that we share together that Jesus will be seen and heard effectively.

We the Baptised have work to do

We are baptised for a purpose: to be a sign of that Word from God which says that God loves the world, that God is met in the circumstances of our daily lives, and that our future belongs to God. We are called to give a name to that mystery which permeates life wherever it is to be found and which will be made known in the fullness of time. This means promoting, cherishing and enabling all that is true, good and beautiful in the human community *(Gaudium et Spes, 76)*; and, at the same time, protesting against injustice, challenging what is inhuman, and siding with the poor and the oppressed.

We the Baptised go forward in hope

We are bearers of the promises of Jesus:

> 'I have come so that they may have life and have it to the full.' *(John 10:10)*
> 'I am the resurrection.' *(John 11:25)*
> 'I am with you always; yes, to the end of time.' *(Matthew 28:20)*
> 'With God on our side who can be against us.' *(Romans 8:31)*

The Baptism of Infants

A Sound Practice?

In our introduction to this chapter, we mentioned that questions are being asked about the suitability of baptising children:

- what possible meaning could baptism have at such an age?
- isn't it more appropriate to delay baptism until a person can decide for himself or herself?

Such questions are only natural in view of the practice of indiscriminate baptism which has given rise to so many non-practising Christians who have no attachment to the Church. Furthermore, with the introduction of RCIA, the Church looks upon adult baptism and the need for personal faith as the norm.

Despite all this, however, we have seen that the practice of infant baptism does have considerable justification:

- the attitude of Jesus towards children;
- it has been the practice of the Church since New Testament times;
- the instinct of parents to embrace their children with love from the moment of conception;
- God's love is not dependent on personal faith.

For these reasons the Church continues to take a firm line in practice in favour of baptising infants. Indeed, in the *Instruction on Infant Baptism*, the Church explicitly counsels against refusing baptism in such

circumstances. We must, therefore, look at ways of celebrating this form of the sacrament in a fruitful way within our parishes.

© *Catholic Pictorial*

The Celebration of Infant Baptism

■ Blessing of Expectant Parents

As with the RCIA, the most important quality of the Christian community is that it be a *welcoming* community. This must begin not with baptism, but with acceptance of the child in the early stages of pregnancy. And so, in a number of parish communities, this is expressed by having a blessing of expectant parents at a specially designated Mass. This enables parents to establish a close personal relationship with their unborn child, for the love of parents is the single most important thing that children pick up in the womb. Sensitivity to such moments within family life will enable the parish community to give necessary support also to those who experience childlessness, miscarriages or still-births.

■ Rite of Welcoming

Once the child is born it is recommended that an opening Rite of Welcoming the child, parents and sponsors should be celebrated as soon as possible. As with the catechumens after the Rite of Entry, the child will now be a member of the household of the faith, but not fully initiated until the moment of baptism.

■ Preparation for Baptism

A suitable period of preparation should now follow for the parents and godparents. This will vary in length according to individual family needs. Parents who are deeply involved in the parish life and community and are strong in the faith will not need the same length of time as parents who are weak in the faith and have little or no appreciation of their responsibility as Christian parents. In these circumstances, we must always exercise great sensitivity, remembering the Lord's acceptance of the prophecy of Isaiah:

'He will not break the crushed reed, nor put out the smouldering wick.'

Matthew 12:20

In a number of parishes, preparation involves about four or five evenings prior to the baptism and is led by the priest in co-operation with religious, catechists, and parents. Without the priest's active support such a programme would lack credibility; without the ministry of catechists and parents it would fail to reflect the Church as the body of Christ with its many gifts. The course will primarily be concerned with enabling parents to recognise their responsibilities in handing on their faith to their children and will conclude with an explanation of the baptismal ceremony. A popular resource is *The Veritas Pre-Baptism Programme: Handing on our Faith* by Mickey and Terri Quinn. One striking development in this connection is that, in some parishes, one of the sessions is held jointly with other local Christian Churches who are also preparing parents for the baptism of their children.

■ Completion of the Baptismal Rite

The Church now encourages that the baptism itself should be celebrated in the context of the Sunday Mass when the parish community would be able to welcome its new members. Some parents, however, for one reason or another, feel uncomfortable with this suggestion, and such feelings must be respected. But, baptism should never be simply a *private* celebration. It is in the faith of the Church that children are baptised and therefore, in addition to parents, godparents, relatives and friends, members of the local community should be represented when the sacrament is celebrated.

Continuing contact with parents after baptism is important, assuring them of all the support they need in bringing up their children within the community of faith. Such support often includes social events for the families of children baptised during the previous year. In so many ways, infant baptism can provide a vital focal point of that call to conversion which is required of the whole parish community.

© Carlos Reyes

Further Reading

Davis, Charles. *The Making of a Christian*, Sheed and Ward, 1964

Dunning, James B. *New Wine: New Wineskins*, Sadlier, 1981

Eastman, A. Theodore. *The Baptising Community*, Seabury Press, 1982

Kavanagh, Aidan. *The Shape of Baptism*, Pueblo Pub. Co. Inc., 1978

Marsh, Thomas A. *Gift of Community*, Michael Glazier, 1984

Quinn, Mickey and Terri. *The Veritas Pre-Baptism Programme*, Veritas, 1984

Rite of Christian Initiation of Adults, Catholic Truth Society, 1974

Whitaker, E.C. *Documents of the Baptismal Liturgy*, SPCK, 1960

CONFIRMATION

Introduction: What is Confirmation?

After all that is said about the importance of the sacrament of baptism, many Catholics wonder about what possible significance can be given to confirmation:

What does it add to our baptism?

Should it once again form part of the sacrament of baptism as was the practice in the early Church?

Is it a sacrament of commitment? A sacrament of Christian maturity, symbolising an awakening of personal faith?

Is it a sacrament for young people, enabling them to cope with the difficult passage of adolescence?

These various questions only reflect the many different understandings of confirmation within the Church today. Inevitably, they give rise to variations in practice concerning the best time to celebrate this sacrament.

Why do these differences exist? How did they come about? What values are they seeking to preserve? These are just some of the questions we need to bear in mind as we retrace our steps and seek to uncover some of the riches intended by Jesus through this sacrament. Before examining the complex history of confirmation we will take a look at some of its biblical roots. Only then shall we be in a position to understand its significance for today.

Biblical Roots of Confirmation

All the sacraments are intended to draw us into communion with the life-giving Spirit of God, but confirmation is traditionally described as the sacrament of the Spirit. In considering its biblical roots, then, we must concentrate on major themes associated with the Spirit in the Scriptures.

The Creative Spirit of God

We first meet the Spirit of God at the very beginning of the Bible. The whole of creation takes place under the presidency of the hovering Spirit of God when the waters of chaos are transformed into the wonders of creation. In the second creation story, the creation of man is the climax when God breathes his own breath into him so that he becomes a living being *(Genesis 2:7)*. From that moment, the Spirit of God is always at work in nature, in history, in human living; and wherever there is a breakdown in God's handiwork, he is present to renew and create again.

'You set springs gushing in ravines,
running down between the mountains,
supplying water for wild animals...
you make fresh grass grow for cattle
and those plants made use of by man,
for them to get food from the soil...
you turn your face away, they suffer,
you stop their breath, they die
and revert to dust.
You give breath, fresh life begins,
you keep renewing the world.'
(Psalm 104:10,15,28-30)

The Prophetic Spirit of God

This same Spirit, at work in the whole of creation, makes its presence felt in the lives of individuals. Moses meets God at the top of the mountain in the midst of a storm *(Exodus 19:18)*; Elijah, on the other hand, finds God in a tiny whispering sound *(1 Kings 19:9-13)*. The great prophets are conscious of being possessed by the Spirit, enabling them to speak the truth of God with clarity of vision and great courage in the face of personal danger and, not infrequently, death itself. It is from the prophet Ezekiel that we receive the most dramatic vision of the power of the Spirit:

> 'Prophesy over these bones. Say, "Dry bones, hear the word of Yahweh. The Lord Yahweh says this to these bones: I am now going to make the breath enter you, and you will live. I shall put sinews on you, I shall make flesh grow on you, I shall cover you with skin and give you breath, and you will live; and you will learn that I am Yahweh".'
>
> *Ezekiel 37:4-6*

The Spirit of Jesus Christ

The New Testament continues this theme of the life-giving Spirit, first in relation to Jesus, and after his death and resurrection, in relation to his followers. In Luke, the mother of Jesus is overshadowed by the Spirit *(Luke 1:35)*. Her barren womb resembles the chaos over which the Spirit hovered when God first uttered his creative word. It is by the power of the same Spirit that Jesus returns from the desert and begins his public ministry:

> 'The Spirit of the Lord has been given to me...to bring the good news to the poor, to proclaim liberty to captives and to the blind new sight, to set the downtrodden free.'
>
> (Luke 4:18-19)

Jesus was conscious of the mission that his Father had given him. He is under no illusion: his mission inevitably involves death. He knew that he was not to have a good death; it would involve a sense of failure, betrayal and rejection, and abandonment. His death on the cross symbolises total helplessness, impossibility in its most acute and final form. And yet, because Jesus remained totally faithful to his Father's will, the Spirit once more, and this time definitively, transforms chaos into life. Jesus, crucified in weakness, is raised by the Spirit of God.

The Spirit of Pentecost

For the disciples, with the death of Jesus, God was dead; they were men for whom God had no further meaning and for whom death alone reigned *(Luke 24:20)*. Once again, only the Spirit of God could bring about a new beginning after such a disastrous end. Luke describes this transformation in the coming of the Holy Spirit on the Apostles in the form of fire. The Pentecostal experience *(Acts 2:1-4)* meant that fire entered into the disciples with the coming of the Spirit, a fire of such intensity that their lives were dramatically transformed, and they became courageous witnesses for Christ.

Experience of the Spirit

If the imagery of fire so quickly came to mind, it is not surprising that the early Christians should speak so naturally of the Spirit living and working amongst them. When the Christians in Jerusalem prayed for courage to speak the Gospel message,

> '...the house where they were assembled rocked; they were all filled with the Holy Spirit and began to proclaim the word of God boldly.'
>
> (Acts 4:31)

The Spirit is recognised immediately in the tremendous transformation that it brought about in people's lives:

> 'I never stop thanking God for all the graces you have received through Jesus Christ. I thank him that you have been enriched in so many ways, especially in your teachers and preachers; the witness to Christ has indeed been strong among you so that you will not be without any of the gifts of the Spirit while you are waiting for our Lord Jesus Christ to be revealed.'
>
> (1 Corinthians 1:4-8)

Above all, the Spirit enabled them to experience God's overwhelming love for them:

> 'The Spirit you received is not the spirit of slaves bringing fear into your lives again; it is the spirit of sons, and it makes us cry out, "Abba, Father".'
>
> (Romans 8:15-16)

With St Paul, the whole of the New Testament witness confirms the Spirit as a living, experienced fact which could not be denied. They came to know as they had never known before the personal presence of God in the Spirit of Jesus Christ.

Receiving the Spirit

Soon after the experience of Pentecost, baptism was recognised to be the sign of a person's acceptance of the message of Christ and his life-giving Spirit. But there are a number of references in the Acts of the Apostles to the laying-on of hands: and so in *Acts 8:14-17*, after the conversion of a number of people in Samaria, Peter and John went there and prayed for the Samaritans to receive the Holy Spirit.

> 'For as yet he had not come down on any of them: they had only been baptised in the name of the Lord Jesus. Then they laid hands on them, and they received the Holy Spirit.'
>
> *Acts 8:16-17*

The laying-on of hands
(Acts 8:14-17)

'They are led by us to a place where there is water...they are then washed...in the water in the Name of the Father and Lord God of all things, and of our Saviour Jesus Christ, and of the Holy Spirit...'

(Apologia 61)

About fifty years later, in 200, Tertullian describes the practice in North Africa where it is clear that a number of ceremonies have been added to the simple rite of washing:

'Then having come up from the font we are thoroughly anointed with a blessed unction...In the next place the hand is laid on in blessing, invoking and inviting the Holy Spirit.'

(On Baptism, cc.7,8)

The Role of the Bishop

Just a few years later, about the year 215, in the writings of Hippolytus, we have the first mention of the special part played by the bishop in the process of initiation. After the rite of washing, the bishop extended a hand over the candidates and prayed that they be filled with the Holy Spirit. Then he poured consecrated oil and laid his hand on their head, made the sign of the cross on their forehead, and gave them the kiss of peace. This part of the rite was eventually to become the sacrament of confirmation.

During the first four or five centuries, therefore, the process of Christian initiation evolved from a simple rite of washing to a more complex ceremony of prayers, washings, anointings, and other symbolic actions culminating in the celebration of the Eucharist. The presence of the bishop was gradually considered to be vitally important because he represented not only the local community but also the wider Church the newly baptised were joining. However, the bishops could not cope with the number of baptisms and, in the West, this had serious consequences for the process of Christian initiation.

A little later, in *Acts 19:1-7*, St Paul finds people at Ephesus who had only received John's baptism, and had not heard that there was a Holy Spirit. They are then baptised in the name of the Lord Jesus and the Holy Spirit comes down upon them when Paul lays his hands on them, and they begin to speak in tongues and to prophesy.

In the New Testament, therefore, baptism refers to the whole process of Christian initiation:

the forgiveness of sins,

becoming children of God,

and receiving the Spirit.

But there are a few indications that there were other ways of receiving the Spirit and these could form the basis of later developments. The Spirit blows where it wills and cannot easily be contained within any single rite.

Gradual Emergence of Confirmation

One Process of Initiation

As the history of baptism shows, initially there was just one process of initiation, incorporating what we now refer to as the three sacraments of baptism, confirmation, and Eucharist. There was no second rite corresponding to what we call confirmation today. Indeed, we have to wait for three centuries before such a pattern emerges.

St Justin describes the practice in Rome about the year AD 150 in the following terms:

Emergence of Confirmation as Separate Rite

In 416, Pope Innocent I had laid down that only the bishops, as successors of the apostles, could anoint with chrism. But, because of the growth of the Church and its extension from town to country, it was impossible for the bishop to be present at all baptisms within his territory. The East and the West approached this problem in different ways:

• in the East, the original unity of the three sacraments was kept in tact by allowing priests to administer confirmation. This is still the Eastern practice and so even infants are given communion after their baptism and confirmation;

• in the West, confirmation remained the preserve of the bishop as head of the local Christian community.

Insistence on this inevitably led to an increasing separation of baptism and confirmation from the fourth century onwards. Nevertheless, up to the twelfth century, the three sacraments were given together, both to infants and adults, whenever a bishop was available.

Furthermore, following the teaching of St Augustine, the Church gradually insisted on baptism taking place as soon as possible after birth. This meant that the majority of baptisms were now performed at churches other than the episcopal cathedral. At the same time, it was felt that confirmation should only be received between the ages of 10 and 14, when children could distinguish between right and wrong.

Finally, in 1910, Pius X encouraged children to receive communion at the age of seven which meant that the original unity of the process of Christian initiation was now lost. Confirmation had now been detached from its baptismal and eucharistic context and left to stand on its own. Catholics received communion before confirmation and so the question naturally arose: if the Eucharist is the sacrament whereby we are made full members of the Church, what is the point of confirmation? Recent developments are all concerned with providing an answer to that question.

Basic Approaches to Confirmation

Out of many possible approaches, Ernest Sands, on a tape presentation entitled *Confirmation*, highlights the following:

Confirmation confers the Holy Spirit

Confirmation has often been traditionally understood as the sacrament which confers the Holy Spirit. This truth is clear from the rite itself. There is the ancient invocation of the Holy Spirit which mentions each of the seven gifts. Both the anointing with chrism and the laying-on of hands symbolises our being sealed with the Spirit of Christ. After the anointing, there follows a prayer which refers to Pentecost and to the coming of the Holy Spirit into the hearts of those just confirmed. And so the connection of confirmation with the Holy Spirit is undeniable. However, the relationship of this sacrament to the Spirit must not be understood in any exclusive way. We know that, in baptism, we become temples of the Holy Spirit and that, in the Eucharist, we are drawn into communion with one another by the Spirit of Christ. Indeed, all the sacraments, in various ways, grant to us a share in the life of the Spirit. We need to be more specific, therefore, about our participation in the Spirit through confirmation. It is not easy, but, perhaps, the best we can say is that through confirmation we are called to be witnesses of Jesus Christ. It is our personal Pentecost.

Confirmation strengthens the Christian

We are familiar with the teaching that confirmation is a sacrament of strength. Many of us will remember the catechism answer that confirmation makes us *'strong and perfect Christians and soldiers of Jesus Christ'*. This represents a tradition which goes back to the fifth century:

> *'In baptism we are born to new life, after baptism we are confirmed for combat. In baptism we are washed, after baptism we are strengthened.'*
> (Faustus of Riez, 460)

Christians needed the assistance of confirmation to face the conflicts and battles of the world and, since the thirteenth century, this has been reflected in the rite with the bishop's slap on the cheek. But, once again, this aspect does not belong to confirmation alone; baptism marks the opening of our warfare with Satan, and this is the meaning of the exorcism and the anointing we receive before baptism. Indeed, all the sacraments prepare us to be active witnesses of Jesus Christ, able to face with courage all the challenges that come our way.

Confirmation is a Sacrament of Commitment and Maturity

This understanding of the sacrament has gained much currency in recent times, when a later age for confirmation is frequently being recommended. Many Catholics look back rather regretfully on their own confirmation, remembering that it had very little meaning for them at the time. Far better that it be given at a time when a person is able to understand what is happening and has some inkling of what an adult Christian commitment means. It is entirely appropriate that God should give us a sacrament that corresponds to this stage in our development when we are able to own our faith in a personal way and actively participate in the life of the Church. But such an understanding cannot exhaust the meaning of confirmation.

For centuries, the sacrament was given to infants and this still is the practice within the Eastern tradition. The significance of confirmation, therefore, must be able to embrace both traditions which reflect quite a difference of approach to the sacrament. To limit the meaning of this sacrament to the sphere of personal commitment and maturity would be an impoverishment and a distortion.

Confirmation completes Baptism

Once confirmation ceased to be part of the rite of baptism, it was difficult to see why it was needed. As a result many people were not confirmed at all. It is within this context that bishops, in the thirteenth century, urged the necessity of confirmation and even imposed penalties for parents who neglected their duty. Such a reaction only reflected a conviction deep within Christian tradition: confirmation represents a vital step in the process of Christian initiation; something is missing if one is not confirmed. But, here too there is more that we must say: not only confirmation, but all the sacraments, especially the Eucharist, help to bring our baptism to completion. The most important way, however, of reaffirming our baptism is by responding faithfully to the call of Christ in the context of our daily lives.

The Celebration of Confirmation

When should Confirmation be celebrated?

■ Immediately after Baptism

Following the example of the Eastern tradition, many would argue that the only way to restore the meaning and status of confirmation is by having, once again, a unified celebration of baptism and confirmation, followed by first reception of communion. This would seem to be the inescapable conclusion of Rite of Christian Initiation of Adults:

> '*According to the ancient practice maintained in the Roman liturgy, an adult is not to be baptised unless he receives confirmation immediately afterward, provided no serious obstacles exist. This connection signifies the unity of the paschal mystery, the close relationship between the mission of the Son and the pouring out of the Holy Spirit, and the joint celebration of the sacraments by which the Son and the Spirit come with the Father upon those who are baptised.*'
>
> (no.34)

The point made here is so important that it should apply not only to adults and teenage children, but to infants as well. The question of age should only affect baptism. And so, if it is right to baptise infants, then, they should be confirmed at the same time. This would mean that, although the bishop is the 'original' minister of confirmation, priests would be the normal ministers of confirmation in our parishes.

■ In Early Adolescence

Approaching the question psychologically and pastorally, however, many people argue that a child should not receive confirmation until the age of 13 or so. The main argument for this point of view would be the desirability of full participation in a sacrament which is given only once. We know how deeply a person's identity is shaped during these years and how faith needs to be confirmed at this age. At the present time, for example, it is well known that a great number of young people, who have been baptised as infants and are supposed to have had a Christian education, are leaving the Church. In such circumstances, those who do not wish to leave might feel the need to make some public act of commitment,

claiming their faith as their own and responding generously to the call of Christ to be his disciples.

Such an understanding, however, does not mean that children should be excluded from the Eucharist until the moment of their confirmation. It is by sharing in the worship of the Christian community, even though only passively, that children learn to pray and come to know something of what it means to be a Christian. On receiving confirmation, such children begin to take part in the Eucharist in a new way, associating themselves personally with the death and resurrection of Jesus.

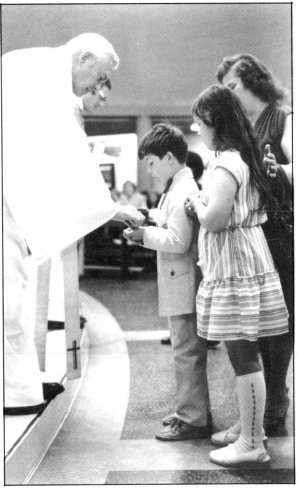

© Carlos Reyes

■ A Plea for Variation

Around the Catholic world, there is no uniform age for confirmation, and this could be due entirely to the work of the Spirit! As we have seen, the sacrament has had quite a chequered history and during that time it has experienced considerable variation. There is no reason why it should not experience similar variations in our own time. We belong to a worldwide Church in which there is considerable variety of social and cultural situations demanding quite different pastoral approaches. In this way, confirmation would always reflect a fundamental characteristic of the Spirit of God: 'it blows where it wills'.

Preparation for Confirmation

Inevitably, the style of preparation will vary depending on the circumstances; the following suggestions have in mind those receiving confirmation in early adolescence:

■ Involve the Whole Parish

Responsibility for ensuring adequate preparation for the sacrament of confirmation lies with the parish, in partnership with the school and the home.

■ Need for Close Co-operation

This will involve close co-operation between the priest, parents, sponsors, catechists, and teachers within the school. The school should ensure that the teaching on confirmation and the Holy Spirit is carried out in the weeks leading up to the celebration of the sacrament. The parish should know what is being taught in the school and develop its own complementary programme.

■ Inaugural Mass, with Enrolment

About two months or so prior to confirmation, it is recommended that candidates, together with their parents and godparents, be invited to an inaugural Mass, when the names of those to be confirmed will be enrolled in a special register. Although it has been customary in the past to choose a special confirmation name, it is now recommended that the baptismal name be used. This enrolment will only be done on the basis of free choice, fully respecting the consciences of the young people to be confirmed. Any undue pressure at this stage will only prove to be counter-productive.

■ Basic Elements of Parish Programme

This will normally take place over a period of six weeks, during which time the young people will be encouraged to recognise their own status as individuals within the Church, with their own particular gifts of the Spirit. Parents, in their turn, will be enabled to provide necessary support for the developing faith of their children. At this time, however, it is important that there are people outside the family whom children admire and to whom they can turn with full confidence because of the personal example of their lives. Ideally, such are the people chosen to be godparents, but the parish itself should be full of people who provide marvellous examples of what it means to be alive in the Spirit. Special emphasis will be given during this time to the importance of prayer and the need to give active witness to our faith in Christ by responding generously to the needs of the local community. It is a time for remembering the words of Jesus:

> 'You are the light of the world. A city built on a hill-top cannot be hidden. No one lights a lamp to put it under a tub; they put it on the lampstand where it shines for everyone in the house. In the same way your light must shine in the sight of men, so that seeing your good works, they may give the praise to your Father in heaven.'
>
> *Matthew 5:14-16*

© Carlos Reyes

■ The Role of the Catechist

The success of parish programmes depends largely on the quality of catechists available to lead the weekly meetings. They need to be people with sufficient self-confidence to lead groups in their reflection upon the meaning of Christian faith. This will obviously entail the basic qualities of sensitivity, compassion, a willingness to listen, and a great deal of patience. But a period of training will also be necessary, depending on the degree of a person's commitment to the ministry. It may be a short course involving specific training for a confirmation programme or a more broadly based form of training, enabling a person to become a leading catechist within a parish. Such a ministry is of vital importance within our parish communities today when adult Christian formation is placed so high on the agenda.

© Carlos Reyes

The Rite of Confirmation

■ Involvement of the Young People

The celebration of confirmation must involve the active participation of the young people to be confirmed. On the same tape referred to earlier, Ernest Sands gives a few suggestions of the kind of thing that can be done:

☆ colour can be given to the setting of the Mass by means of posters, banners, and, perhaps, a collage, prepared by the children, highlighting different aspects of the significance of confirmation;

☆ the theme of the Mass can be introduced by one of the children;

☆ a group of children can be responsible for leading the congregation in the penitential rite;

☆ naturally, the readings will be done by the children; only the Gospel reading is necessary and for that the children may do a mime;

☆ the Bidding Prayers should also be in the hands of the children; and the procession of gifts might include tokens of various aspects of their life, including, perhaps, money raised from sponsored events, to emphasise the notion of witness;

☆ and finally, a Eucharistic Prayer for children.

■ The Laying-on of Hands

After the renewal of baptismal promises and the profession of faith, the bishop, together with his assistant priests, extends his hands over those who are to be confirmed. This gesture, used in a wide variety of contexts, symbolises a person being empowered in the Spirit. The bishop adds significance to the gesture because, as leader of the local Church, he above all bears the responsibility for commissioning new apostles of the Gospel. As he does so, he says the following prayer:

> 'My dear friends: in baptism God our Father gave the new birth of eternal life to his chosen sons and daughters. Let us pray to our Father that he will pour out the Holy Spirit to strengthen his sons and daughters with his gifts and anoint them to be more like Christ the Son of God.
> All powerful God, Father of our Lord Jesus Christ, by water and the Holy Spirit you freed your sons and daughters from sin and gave them new life. Send your Holy Spirit upon them to be their helper and guide. Give them the spirit of wisdom and understanding, the spirit of right judgement and courage, the spirit of knowledge and reverence. Fill them with the spirit of wonder and awe in your presence. We ask this through Christ our Lord.'

[Illustrations on pages 26 and 27: some examples of the ways in which young people are involved in the life of the Church.]

■ Anointing with Chrism

The bishop now dips his right thumb in chrism and makes the sign of cross on the forehead of each person to be confirmed. *Chrism* is an oil which is mixed with perfume symbolising that Christians should be the pleasant fragrance of Christ in the world and that they themselves should experience friendship with God as a beautiful thing. *The Sign of the Cross* is the sign of Christ and symbolises his promise to be utterly faithful to us; he will never go back on his word. As the bishop anoints with chrism, he mentions the person by name and says: *'Be sealed with the Gift of the Holy Spirit'.*

© Catholic Pictorial

■ Eucharist as Climax of Christian Initiation

The celebration of the Eucharist continues. Of course, the young children will have been receiving communion for a number of years. But the Eucharist, following immediately upon confirmation, is special. It marks the beginning of taking part in the Eucharist in a new way. Now, the young children will always be reminded of the responsibility that is theirs of sharing in the mission of Jesus, responding generously to the needs of others. It is most appropriate that the children receive communion under both kinds.

At the final blessing at the end of Mass, the bishop prays over the people:

'God our Father, complete the work you have begun and keep the gifts of your Holy Spirit active in the hearts of your people. Make them ready to live his Gospel and eager to do his will. May they never be ashamed to proclaim to all the world Christ crucified living and reigning for ever and ever.'

What Kind of Church confirms?

A Church alive to the Gifts of the Spirit

A Church which confirms is, first of all, alive to the immense richness of the gifts of the Spirit. We are familiar with the basic gifts of the Spirit:

love: welcoming the rich possibilities in the lives of others;

joy: the exuberance which comes from living truly creative lives;

patience: the willingness to listen and to give time for one another;

kindness: a readiness to be attentive to the needs of others;

goodness: the ability to make friends easily and to draw out what is best in others;

faithfulness: a strong faith in God and one upon whom others can depend for support and encouragement;

gentleness: slow to judge and condemn, but rich in mercy and compassion;

self-control: not afraid of the high ideals of the Gospel.

'The Gifts of the Spirit'.

Such are the gifts which should provide a natural setting for confirmation.

Unfortunately, many of us have what can be called a 'winter-time' experience of the faith — a life of faith which is largely under the surface and rarely blossoms into a vivid awareness of the presence of God. We tend to accept such an experience as the norm with the result that we rarely taste that sense of joy which Jesus promised to his disciples. How refreshing, then, are the words of Pope Paul VI:

> 'The authentic Christian faith which we profess has to be lived with enthusiasm. Enthusiasm is a flame which so many contrary winds today try to extinguish. Where is the enthusiasm of our faith today? There are no doubt many living members of the Church — a great many — who live and feel this joyous and generous enthusiasm. To these brothers and sisters, let us now give our greeting and blessing, like a breath of Pentecost.'

© Carlos Reyes

A Church which takes seriously the Spirit in Everyone

Within the Church, we must recognise that the Spirit of God speaks through everyone: through the poor and the young just as much as through the rich and the old, through men and women, through simple people and through scholars and experts. Even though all may have different capacities, desires or abilities, beyond all these diversities everyone shares in the one Spirit. Centuries ago Jeremiah proclaimed the words of Yahweh in the following terms:

> 'Deep within them I will plant my Law, writing it on their hearts. Then I will be their God and they shall be my people. There will be no further need for neighbour to try to teach neighbour, or brother to say to brother, "Learn to know Yahweh!" No, they will all know me, the least no less than the greatest — it is Yahweh who speaks — since I will forgive their iniquity and never call their sin to mind.'
>
> (Jeremiah 31:33-34)

This prophecy finds fulfilment in the New Testament which describes the presence of the Spirit of Christ within us as an inner illumination, opening our hearts to the Gospel:

> 'It is the same God that said, "Let there be light shining out of darkness", who has shone in our minds to radiate the light of the knowledge of God's glory, the glory on the face of Christ.'
>
> (2 Corinthians 4:6)

Because we belong together in the Spirit of Jesus Christ, we are called upon especially to breathe new life into one another, to create an experience of friendship in our relationship with one another, to draw out from one another what is best in each of us. Only in this way will we help one another to be *confirmed* in the Spirit. Too often, we take one another for granted and encourage a spirit of criticism and cynicism which only serves to destroy any possibility of genuine friendship and mutual respect. We must rather set free the gifts that belong to each of us, especially to the young who, if encouraged, will bring with them a breath of fresh air and new ideas. Mutual respect and understanding does not come easily and will inevitably mean facing the need to struggle, to grow, to change, to risk, to be creative, and to have patience. Such, however, is the challenge of the Spirit!

A Church committed to Evangelisation

As Christians, confirmed in the Spirit, we are called to be witnesses to the Gospel of Jesus Christ, instinctively sharing with others what we ourselves have received. This means, first of all, possessing a deeply rooted conviction of being totally accepted and cherished by God as Father; recognising Jesus as the Lord of our life: 'Be brave, I have conquered the world' *(John 16:33)*; and experiencing the Spirit praying within, bringing alive the love that comes from Father and Son.

In the Spirit, the risen Lord is present; the Gospel is no longer a dead letter but the power of life; the Church is a communion of believers made one by the

Father, the Son and Holy Spirit; the liturgy is truly an occasion for celebration. This vivid awareness of the Father, of Jesus as Lord, and of the Spirit, brings home in a remarkable way the love, care, guidance, power, mercy and providence of God. No evangelisation is possible without such personal conversion:

> *'The world is calling for evangelisers to speak to it of a God whom the evangelists themselves should know and be familiar with as if they could see the invisible.'*
>
> (Pope Paul VI, On Evangelisation, no.76)

But, when we look on the world, broken by suffering of every kind, we can be overcome by a feeling of helplessness. Each of us has our own particular concerns of work, mortgage, examinations, bringing up children, and the cost of living. How can we respond in a practical way to the many global issues that cry out for our attention: world poverty, world hunger and starvation, world inflation, over-population, pollution, the arms race? The list is endless. It needs the genius of a Bob Geldof or of a parish such as The Parish of Our Lady of the Wayside, Birmingham, to bring these issues within the common reach of ordinary people like ourselves.

We are only too familiar with the remarkable inspiration of Bob Geldof in bringing home to us the needs of the starving peoples of Africa. The story of the parish in Birmingham is told by its parish priest, Fr Paddy O'Mahony, in a pamphlet entitled, *One Parish — One World: One Parish and Human Rights* (Catholic Truth Society). He writes of a parish which offers a marvellous example of incorporating a human rights programme with the continuing day-to-day life of the parish. Weekly Masses always include a prayer for those suffering violation of their rights. Even the vestments, the design of the Church building and its furnishings reflect a passion for human dignity. Without neglecting responsibilities at home, the parish has still managed to send thousands of pounds' worth of medicines and equipment to countries in the Third World as well as building up resources for providing immediate relief in cases of disaster.

In speaking at Coventry of the need for world peace, John Paul II has pointed the way forward when faced with seemingly insuperable problems:

© *Solihull News*

Father Paddy O'Mahony of Our Lady of the Wayside, Birmingham, discusses medical supplies for Poland.

Further Reading

Cunningham, Joseph L. *Confirmation: Pastoral Concerns,* The Liturgical Press (Collegeville), 1972

Harrington, Wilfrid. *Spirit of the Living God*, Michael Glazier, 1977

Kiesling, Christopher. *Confirmation*, Messenger Press, 1973

Milner, Austin P. *Theology of Confirmation*, Mercier, 1972

O'Connor, Edward D. *Pope Paul and the Spirit*, Ave Maria Press, 1978

Ramsey, Michael. *Holy Spirit*, SPCK, 1977

Rite of Confirmation, ICEL, 1971

Sands, Ernest. *Sacrament of Confirmation*, Unitape, 1983 [audiotape]

'The cathedral of peace is built of many small stones. Each person has to become a stone in that beautiful edifice...Mistrust and division between nations begin in the hearts of individuals. Work for peace starts when we listen to the urgent call of Christ: "Repent and believe in the gospel".'

EUCHARIST

Differing Attitudes to the Eucharist

The Eucharist has been seen by Catholics through the centuries as the central action of the Church: 'the source and summit of all Christian life' (*Constitution on the Liturgy*, 10). We are familiar with the phrase, 'It is the Mass that matters'.

Inevitably, therefore, there have been strong feelings about the many changes we have been experiencing in recent years:

- many are able to rejoice over the changes: the use of English, the opportunity for active participation, more frequent communion, reception of communion in the hand, communion under both kinds; all have served to give a sense of belonging within the Church they have never experienced before;

- others, especially amongst the young, have reacted quite differently: 'why should I go to Mass on Sunday, since, despite the changes, it is still so boring?'; 'it doesn't seem to have any relevance for my daily life'; 'very few of my friends go, so why should I?'

- some older people regret the passing of the Latin Mass and a loss of that sense of reverence and mystery which belonged to the old Mass; and what has happened, they ask, to Benediction and the processions of the Blessed Sacrament?

To approach these and many other questions we need to reflect on the intentions of Christ when he gave us the Eucharist and on the way in which this gift has been understood by the Church over the centuries.

The Eucharist as Gift from the Lord

'For this is what I received from the Lord, and in turn passed on to you; that on the same night he was betrayed, the Lord Jesus took some bread, and thanked God for it and broke it, and he said, "This is my body which is for you; do this as a memorial of me". In the same way, he took the cup after supper, and said, "This cup is the new covenant in my blood. Whenever you drink it, do this as a memorial of me".'
(1 Corinthians 11:23-35; cf. Matthew 26:26-29; Mark 14:22-25; Luke 22:14-20)

In order to understand this sacrament we must, first of all, try to recall the memories that Jesus was trying to evoke that night before he died and the commitment he was asking of his disciples.

- ▲ The setting was that of Passover, when the Jewish people celebrated their deliverance from Egypt and the everlasting covenant that God has made with them. On this night, Jesus told them, their passover must be in memory of him.

- ▲ The Last Supper was anticipated by a number of meals that Jesus had shared with sinners and tax-collectors. When asked why he did this, Jesus replied: *'It is not the healthy who need the doctor but the sick...I did not come to call the virtuous but sinners'* (Matthew 9:12-13). Such meals symbolised the compassion, the risking, the reaching-out, the total caring that so marked the life of Jesus. He had lived for the lost, for sinners, now he would die for them.

- ▲ At the Last Supper, Jesus indicated how this love would reach its fulfilment. *'This is my body given for you...This is my blood shed for you...Do this in memory of me.'* With these words, Jesus embraced his death upon the cross. He would experience betrayal and denial, he would be jeered and mocked, he would experience even abandonment by the Father, 'but now he showed how perfect his love was' *(John 13:1)*. In his death, he made known the measure of the love of God reaching out to all.

- ▲ But such love would not remain just a distant memory. The love of the risen Lord, shaped by his sacrifice on the cross, would always be present

to us and, in a special way, in our celebration of the Eucharist. As with the disciples on the road to Emmaus, Jesus assures us that we will always recognise him *'at the breaking of bread'* (Luke 24:35).

▲ As Jesus expressed his readiness to be broken and poured out to set the world free, his disciples must have experienced something of the commitment he was asking of them. As they raised the cup to their lips, they must have remembered those words of Jesus *'Can you drink the cup that I must drink?'* (Mark 10:38). And again, after washing their feet, Jesus told them: *'I have given you an example, so that you may copy what I have done to you...happiness will be yours if you behave accordingly.'* (John 13:15-17).

▲ This shared love with Jesus in the present is to be the basis of our hope for the future when we shall enjoy his love for ever: *'I tell you solemnly, I shall not drink any more wine until the day I drink the new wine in the kingdom of God.'* (Mark 14:25). Jesus assures us that nothing will ever come between us and our God. Such is the pledge that belongs to the heart of the gift of the Eucharist, a celebration which looks forward to the future, full of confidence and hope.

An Historical Sketch of the Church's Celebration of the Eucharist

First Three Centuries: a Community Celebration

In the beginning, the celebration of the Eucharist naturally followed the pattern of the Last Supper set in the context of an ordinary meal. And so, for example, St Paul, writing to the Corinthians about the year AD 54, warns against abuses which are taking place in such meals, some helping themselves while others were going hungry *(1 Corinthians 10:20)*. Very early in the Church's life, however, the Eucharist was separated from the ordinary meal and consisted simply of those elements to which the Lord had attached special significance.

An early description of the Eucharist is given to us by St Justin, writing in about 150:

'At the conclusion of the prayers, we greet one another with a kiss. Then the bread and a chalice containing wine mixed with water are presented to the one presiding over the brethren. He takes them and offers praise and glory to the Father of all...At the end of these prayers and eucharist, all present express their approval by saying "Amen" ...And when he who presides has made eucharist they whom we call deacons permit each one present to partake of the eucharistised bread, and wine and water; and they carry it also to the absentees.'

(St Justin's Apology)

In these few words, following the liturgy of the Word we have the basic shape of the Eucharist as it was celebrated in the early centuries of the Church:

the Kiss of Peace: a significant moment when everyone is reminded of the Lord's statement *(Matthew 5:34ff)* that one has to be reconciled with one's brothers and sisters if one wishes to bring a gift to the altar;

the Eucharistic Prayer: this prayer developed out of the prayers of blessing in the Old Testament, praising God for all creation, for his powerful acts of liberation in history, for his tremendous generosity, and for his particular kindness to his people in need. Within the Eucharist, all this praise now focuses on Christ. This prayer was reserved to the bishop and was responded to by all the people with their 'Amen'.

Communion: this formed the climax of the celebration. Communion was received by 'all attending' and was generally received under both kinds. It was then taken to those who were unable to be present to draw them into the fellowship of the Christian community.

It was truly a community celebration; there were no idle spectators or listeners; all were actively participating. Possibly because of the prevailing political circumstances of persecution, it was a brief celebration lasting not more than twenty minutes even with quite a number of communicants. But the pattern was soon to change.

'This is my body, given for you.'

The PASSOVER *Celebrated by the* PORTUGUESE JEWS.

Beginning in the Fourth Century: A Change of Direction

The basic change was that, by degrees, the Eucharist was no longer celebrated consciously as an action of the Christian community. This process began as early as the fourth century with a serious decline in the numbers of people receiving communion. On the one hand, people were being constantly warned against the dangers of unworthy communion and the need for right dispositions; on the other hand, the Eucharist itself was described in the most exalted terms because it contained the divine presence of Jesus. It was described by St Cyril, for example, as 'that most terrifying hour'. People were made to feel so anxious that they were frightened of receiving communion. By the ninth century, communion was no longer received on the hand and, when it was received, it was received kneeling. It was only natural in these circumstances that the Fourth Lateran Council, in the thirteenth century, should insist on Easter Communion, referred to popularly as 'one's Easter duties'.

The new focal point was the moment of consecration. Priests began to raise the host above their heads that people might see and adore; bells were rung to attract attention, torches were held so that people could see better and incense was offered. People now spoke in terms of attending and hearing Mass rather than celebrating the Eucharist. The Eucharistic prayer was now said in Latin and was said alone by the priest in silence with his back to the people. It provided an occasion for individual devotion on the part of both

priests and people focused on the adoration of the Lord Jesus in the Blessed Sacrament.

Such a description of the Mass will be familiar to many of us as we reflect back to our own childhood. The priest would have thought it most strange if we had approached the altar rails for communion at the 11 o'clock Mass on Sunday morning. It was taken for granted that Mass could be celebrated without the people receiving communion. We will remember, too, the great silence that would descend on the congregation at the moment of consecration to be followed afterwards with a general shuffling and a spontaneous clearing of the throat! With the Mass in Latin, and the priest's back to the people, the Mass was generally regarded as something 'done' by the priest and 'watched' by the people. In addition, we were familiar with Benediction on Sunday and Thursday evenings, together with Holy Hour, Forty Hours Exposition, and Corpus Christi processions — all of which developed at a time when people rarely received communion as their daily bread. One entry in a parish diary of 40 years ago reads: 'Only 300 at Benediction — Snow'!

But change had to come. The Church was beginning to read the Scriptures afresh, especially those words of Jesus uttered at the Last Supper: *'Take and eat; Take and drink; This is my body given for you; This is my blood shed for you.'* The first step towards renewal, therefore, was Pope Pius X's encouragement in 1910 to receive communion frequently. All the changes that have taken place since that time: the use of English, more active participation, the reception of communion on the hand and under both kinds — all are intended to bring home to us the dignity that is ours in belonging to the body of Christ. In particular, the changes inspired by Vatican II have three aims in view:

- to transform our celebrations of the Eucharist into community celebrations;

- to make our celebrations occasions for listening to God's Word in the Scriptures;

- to promote active participation on the part of the whole community.

Celebrating our Sunday Parish Mass Today

Titles we give to our Sunday Celebration

The most common title for our Sunday celebration is the *Mass* which is derived from the Latin word 'missa' meaning 'sent'. It reminds us of the responsibility that is ours of sharing in the mission of Christ, the sending of Christ. We cannot celebrate Mass Sunday by Sunday and be indifferent to the anguished cries in the world around us.

Because of the richness of the mystery of the Mass, however, no one title can do justice to its meaning. And so a number of other titles are used, the principal ones being as follows:

Christian Passover: emphasises our spiritual origin from Israel and Jesus as the principal means whereby we pass over from death to life;

Lord's Supper: we come together in obedience to the Lord's words: 'Do this in memory of me; Take and eat; Take and drink';

Holy Communion: expresses the extent of our shared life together because of our communion with Christ; in the words of St Paul: 'We are the body of Christ';

Eucharist: we come together to thank God, our Father, for all that he has done for us through his Son, Jesus Christ.

Of all these titles only 'Mass' and 'Eucharist' would normally be used within the Roman Catholic tradition.

The Basic Parts of the Mass

The Mass is made up of two parts, the Liturgy of the Word and the Liturgy of the Eucharist, and these two parts

> '...are so closely connected as to form one single act of worship. The table of God's Word and of Christ's Body is prepared and from it the faithful are instructed and nourished.'
> (The Parish Mass, no.8, p.9)

The **Liturgy of the Word** represents God's invitation to his people to come together for worship. It usually consists of three readings, one from the Old Testament, and two from the New Testament, the final one being a passage from one of the Gospels. Over the period of a three year cycle we receive a comprehensive coverage of the four Gospels, a major part of the rest of the New Testament and a large section of passages from the Old Testament. We need to listen attentively to the word of God and, afterwards, rest in silence for a moment allowing what we have heard to penetrate our hearts. It is a time for remembering the Lord's words: 'Happy are those who hear the word of God and keep it' *(Matthew 11:28).*

© Carlos Reyes

© Carlos Reyes

The **Liturgy of the Eucharist**, which follows, takes its shape from the four-fold action of Jesus at the Last Supper:

he **took** bread and wine;

said the **blessing**;

broke the bread;

and **gave** it to them saying: *'Take and eat. Take and drink.'*

First of all, then, bread and wine are **brought** to the altar in procession by lay people. They carry simple gifts, which might include, in addition to the bread and wine, the collection money and other tokens symbolising our daily lives and the particular service that we render to the Lord.

Then follows the **Blessing**, the Eucharistic Prayer, more popularly referred to as the 'Canon of the Mass'. We thank God, our Father, for the gift of his Son, Jesus Christ, who will soon be giving himself to us under the form of bread and wine. We pray that the Holy Spirit might transform our gifts of bread and wine and so become for us the body and blood of Jesus Christ. We recall the moment of the Last Supper, and especially, the death, resurrection and ascension of Jesus to the right hand of the Father, where he constantly intercedes on our behalf. We pray that, together with Christ, we might offer ourselves to the Father by the power of the same Spirit. We pray, too, for the whole Church, both the living and the dead, confident that we are truly safe in the hand of our God. Finally, we conclude on a note of praise and thanksgiving: 'Through him, with him, in him...' to which we all respond 'Amen'.

Now the **bread is broken**; this is a most important part of our celebration which so often goes unnoticed because we are accustomed to receiving individual hosts. Its meaning is that the one Christ is to be shared by many so that the many might be made one, a theme dear to the heart of St Paul *(1 Corinthians 10:17)*.

Our celebration comes to a climax in the moment of **Communion** when we experience the fulfilment of those words of Jesus: *'He who eats my flesh and drinks my blood lives in me and I live in him.'* (John 6:57). We have the opportunity of receiving in the hand and are encouraged to receive from the chalice in obedience to the Lord's command: 'Take and drink'. Then, with the help of Lay Ministers of Communion, communion is frequently taken to the sick and the housebound, for no one must be isolated within the body of Christ.

© Carlos Reyes

More needs to be said, however, if these basic elements are to come alive in the form of prayerful worship. In particular, we need to know the meaning of the varied symbolism which belongs to the heart of this sacrament.

> 'You are a chosen race, a royal priesthood, a consecrated nation, a people set apart to sing the praises of God who called you out of darkness into his wonderful light.'
>
> *1 Peter 2:9*

Symbolism of the Eucharist

Christian Assembly

The most important symbol is that of the Christian Assembly itself, the gathering of Christians to break bread and give thanks to the Father. Such gatherings vary from simple house Masses, to the large Sunday congregations, to the grand papal celebrations of the Eucharist. But, whatever the size, the essential truth is that the 'Church' is first and foremost the faithful, the gathering of Christians to celebrate the Eucharist. In the words of St Paul: 'We are the Body of Christ'. Christ is the Head and we, the people, are his members. And if such a body is to function then all members must work together for the good of the whole body, for God has 'put all the separate parts into the body on purpose' *(1 Corinthians 12:18)*. This is reflected in our celebration by the variety of ministries: the president, the reader, the cantor, the usher, the lay minister of communion, and, indeed, all of us together playing our part to build up the body of Christ. No one person can do everything for 'the body is not to be identified with any one of its many parts' *(1 Corinthians 12:14)*. In the marvellous words of St Peter:

From earliest times, the Christian assembly has come together on Sunday, the Lord's Day, the day on which Jesus rose from the dead. It also came to represent the first day of creation when God created light. This means that an atmosphere of joy should prevail within the assembly, an atmosphere of hospitality and fellowship, 'each part [of the body] may be equally concerned for all the others' *(1 Corinthians 12:24)*.

Communal Meal

When we come together on the Lord's Day we do so to share a meal together, the Christian Passover meal, the Lord's Supper. In human experience, meals not only provide physical nourishment but can also be a powerful means of binding people together. In acknowledging our need of food, we acknowledge our dependence on other people. The food and drink we share comes from all over the world and depends on the co-operation of millions of people. Sharing the same food and drink opens us to fellowship and creates a special kind of friendship among us. That is why family gatherings and special holidays naturally

© Carlos Reyes

© *Carlos Reyes*

include a festive meal. For Jesus, too, meals were highly significant moments and so it is not surprising that he should choose the setting of a meal to impress upon us his desire to share his life with us and be at home with us.

At this meal, we receive Jesus into our lives under the form of **bread and wine**. Nigel Bavidge, in his booklet on the Eucharist, briefly describes the significance of bread: 'Of all the forms of food, bread is regarded as the most essential, the staff of life. It is easily available and sustains life when all else fails; it was 'manna from heaven' for the people of Israel as they journeyed through the desert. Moreover, to become bread, the wheat must be ground down and crushed to make flour.' Bread, therefore, is a natural symbol for signifying our dependence on Jesus:

> 'I am the bread of life. He who comes to me will never be hungry; he who believes in me will never thirst.'
>
> *John 6:35*

All of these meanings come together as we recognise Jesus in the breaking of bread. But in order not to put too great a strain on our faith, the bread of the Eucharist must bear some resemblance to the bread on the kitchen table! Unfortunately, it is still the thin white wafer which prevails.

In Jesus' time, wine was always served at a meal with friends and it still is one of the most common drinks around the world. It is a symbol of joy and happiness and, for the Jews, a symbol of the abundant blessings of God. We are reminded of the marriage feast at Cana where Jesus came to the aid of the embarrassed newly-married couple by providing 120 gallons of the best wine! The love of God is without measure. And, as with the wheat for the bread, so the grape, too, must be crushed to form the wine. It is only natural, once again, therefore, that Jesus should turn to the symbolism of wine to express the love that he bears for us:

> 'I am the vine, you are the branches.
>
> Whoever remains in me, with me in him, bears fruit in
>
> plenty; for cut off from me you can do nothing.'
>
> *John 15:5*

As we take hold of the chalice, we are reminded, too, of the cup that Jesus had to drink.

In the light of such symbolism, we can appreciate the value of receiving communion under both kinds which is now becoming normal practice in many of our parishes. It is only right that this should be the case:

• it expresses more fully what Jesus did at the Last Supper when he said: 'Take and eat... Take and drink';

• it brings home to us more clearly that the Eucharist is a meal at which one both eats and drinks;

• it emphasises the rich symbolism of the wine as it has been described above: '...my blood, the blood of the covenant, which is to be poured out for many for the forgiveness of sins.' *(Matthew 26:28)*

© Catholic Pictorial

An Act of Thanksgiving to the Father

Each time we gather to celebrate the Eucharist, a word which means thanksgiving, Jesus wants to impress upon all of us the need for a grateful heart. We need to experience the goodness and glory of God so profoundly that we are simply glad to praise him. Jesus wants to draw us back to a fundamental attitude which has characterised prayer to God from the very beginning. The Psalms of the Old Testament are essentially hymns of praise:

'Bless Yahweh, my soul, bless his holy name, all that is in me! Bless Yahweh, my soul, and remember all his kindnesses: in forgiving all your offences, in curing all your diseases...'

(Psalm 103:1-3)

The same is inevitably true of prayer in the New Testament. The mother of Jesus sings her Magnificat: 'My soul glorifies the Lord, my spirit rejoices in God my Saviour' *(Luke 1:46)*; and Jesus himself prays:

'I bless you, Father, Lord of heaven and earth, for hiding these things from the learned and the clever and revealing them to mere children.'

(Luke 10:21)

All this prayer is gathered together in our celebration of Eucharist, the principal focus of our thanksgiving and our praise of God:

> 'We come to you, Father, with praise and
>
> thanksgiving, through Jesus Christ your Son.'
>
> *Roman Canon*

We thank God, above all, for our faith in Jesus; we thank God for our relatives, friends and the many memories that have shaped our lives; we thank God for the faith of one another, echoing the sentiments of John Paul II at Wembley: 'I thank God for the privilege of celebrating the Eucharist with you.' Praise and thanksgiving should be as instinctive to the Christian heart as breathing.

A Memorial of the Sacrifice of Christ

As we celebrate the Eucharist, we remember the death of Jesus on the cross. In that moment, we are able to see the human yearning at the heart of divine love to share himself with men and women in their human and sinful frailty. In the words of St John:

'God loved the world so much that he gave his only Son, so that everyone who believes in him may not be lost but may have eternal life.'

(John 3:16)

The message of the cross says simply: God is with us in our insecurity, anxiety, darkness and guilt. We do not know how to help ourselves, but God is always present as our strength. The name of God is 'God-with-us' and he will enable us to triumph over every situation which seems to threaten us. It is this love of God, this forgiveness and liberation from all anxiety, expressed so dramatically upon the cross, and which alone satisfies the ache of the human heart today, that we celebrate in the Eucharist. This love is made present to us in the person of the risen Lord who is alive and active amongst us and who draws us into the movement of his own self-offering to the Father. He challenges us to become what we are born to become, a people of hope, believing that our sadness and sinfulness have been overcome by the powerful love he has for us.

A Presence of Christ in the Spirit

As we come together, we celebrate the mystery of our unity with one another in the Spirit of Christ. For St Paul, we are so inseparable from the resurrection, that he can only speak of us as the body of Christ. This vision lay at the heart of his Damascus experience: 'Saul, Saul, why are you persecuting me?' *(Acts 9:4)*. As risen Lord, Jesus is present to us now much more intimately than he could have been before his passion and death. It is impossible to imagine the truth he expresses so simply: *'Make your home in me, as I make mine in you.'* (John 15:4).

There are two moments, as we have seen, in our celebration of the Eucharist which bring this marvellous truth home to us. The first is the kiss of peace, a simple gesture, whereby we express our common sharing in the life of Jesus. We are reminded that before approaching the altar we need to be at peace with one another. Perhaps before leaving our church on Sunday morning we might introduce ourselves in a personal way to those with whom we have shared the peace of Christ. So often we come together as strangers when our experience should be one of friendship and acceptance. The second moment is communion itself when we answer 'Amen' to the words 'the body of Christ'. We do not simply mean 'yes, *it is* the body of Christ' but also 'yes, *we are* the body of Christ'. There is a real sense in which we receive one another in receiving Christ in communion. One parish priest is supposed to have remarked: 'Some of my people are going to be very hard to swallow!'

A Sharing in the Mission of Christ

If the Eucharist symbolises food and drink and sharing a meal in the memory of Jesus, we cannot be in-

different to so many millions of people who constantly live with hunger, many of them dying of malnutrition. We cannot celebrate the presence of the Bread of Life without being challenged to do something about this appalling reality. We only receive the bread of life in order to share it with those in need, for the Jesus we receive in communion is the same Jesus who was so passionate in his concern for the poor:

> *'The spirit of the Lord has been given to me, for he has anointed me. He has sent me to bring the good news to the poor, to proclaim liberty to captives and to the blind new sight, to set the downtrodden free, to proclaim the Lord's year of favour.'*
>
> (Luke 4:18)

In calling our Sunday celebration the 'Mass', we must be always conscious that we are called to share in the mission of Jesus, the *sending* of Jesus, so that we ourselves might become the bread of life for those in need. Through us those words of Jesus should sound loud and clear:

> 'Come to me, all you who labour and are overburdened, and I will give you rest. Shoulder my yoke and learn from me, for I am gentle and humble in heart, and you will find rest for your souls. Yes, my yoke is easy and my burden light.'
>
> *Matthew 11:28-30*

© Carlos Reyes

Mgr Thomas Adamson's last Benediction at St Clare's, Liverpool, before his retirement.

© Catholic Pictorial

Devotion to the Blessed Sacrament

Why Benediction?

Rosary, Sermon and Benediction used to be part of our staple devotional diet. How times have changed! With the advent of evening Mass and people voting with their feet on the few occasions Benediction is offered, a whole generation of Catholics is growing up without any experience of Benediction at all.

In view of all that we have said so far, it is only right that the Mass is the primary liturgical means whereby we experience the continuing presence of God in our lives. But just as the act of love between husband and wife requires the support of looks, actions and words, so the Mass is enriched considerably by a strong devotion to the Blessed Sacrament. It provides a marvellous opportunity for simply relaxing in the presence of the risen Lord and spending time contemplating the one who constantly offers himself to us as the food of life. Only in this way will we appreciate that it is the Mass that matters.

In reality, reservation of the Blessed Sacrament, primarily intended for the sick, should express our profound unwillingness for the Mass to end. In the reserved sacrament, we have a most powerful symbol of Christ's abiding presence within the Church constantly offering himself to us as our daily food and drink. Ultimately, devotion to the Blessed Sacrament provides us with the opportunity of adoring and praising God for what he is and for what he has done for us.

The New Rite of Benediction

Although it was as long ago as 1973 that the Vatican promulgated its document on 'Holy Communion and the Worship of the Eucharist outside Mass', it was only in 1979 that it became easily available in England. The new Rite of Benediction is very simple and can easily be adapted to suit the circumstances:

Exposition
Processional Song and Exposition carried out in silence

Adoration
Opening Prayer (setting out the theme of celebration)
Period of Silent Adoration
A Reading from Scripture
Period of Silent Adoration

Benediction
Incensing during Eucharistic Song
Prayer
Blessing

Reposition
Final Song

In addition to this simple rite of Benediction, the New Rite also provides a format for Eucharistic Processions, as well as prayers and readings which could be used at a Holy Hour. It also contains a short catechetical section dealing with the reasons for eucharistic devotion, emphasising the importance for setting the whole eucharistic mystery firmly within the context of our daily life. There can be no doubt that this document, if used to full advantage, will help towards a deep enrichment of people's faith in the Eucharist, especially at a time when there is such an evident hunger for an experience of the closeness of God in the Spirit of Jesus Christ.

Further Reading

Dix, Gregory. *The Shape of the Liturgy*, Dacre Press, n.d.

Guzie, Tad. *Jesus and the Eucharist*, Paulist Press, 1974

Hellwig, Monika K. *The Eucharist and the Hunger of the World*, Paulist Press, 1976

Keifer, Ralph A. *Blessed and Broken*, Michael Glazier, 1982

The Parish Mass, Catholic Truth Society, 1981

Powers, Joseph M. *Eucharistic Theology*, Burns and Oates, 1967

PENANCE & RECONCILIATION

Introduction

Just a few years ago, it was a common scene on Saturdays to have numbers of people going to confession, and these numbers were greatly increased around the time of the major feasts of the year, Christmas and Easter. Indeed, hearing confessions was one of the principal tasks of priests working in parishes.

Confession followed a fairly set routine. We entered the confessional box, to preserve our anonymity, and began by stating how long it was since our last confession. We then gave a list of our sins, saying how often each one had been committed: 'I have missed my morning and night prayers a few times; I have been uncharitable a few times; I have been impure by myself a few times...and that is all Father'. The priest would then give a few words of advice or encouragement, followed by a penance (nearly always a few prayers) to be said after we had left the confessional. We would then say an act of contrition, after which the priest would pronounce the words of absolution. The whole experience would only last a few minutes and yet it has generated a great deal of fear in the hearts of many Catholics from early childhood: what shall I say? how will the priest react? what will he think?

Quite a number of people still depend on frequent confession in the form they have always been accustomed to throughout their lives. It is important pastorally that such people who wish to continue as in the past, should be allowed to do so. Many other people, however, now receive the sacrament of confession much less frequently — once or twice a year — if that often. It isn't, necessarily, that such people are less good or less devout than they were. It is just that growing numbers of people no longer look on the traditional pattern of confession as being central to their Christian lives. This change has happened very rapidly and a number of reasons could be given:

— there has been a decline in the sense of sin and in the need for forgiveness; a failure to confess is in line with a lack of faith and a failure to pray;

— frequent confession, however, did promote an unhealthy self-image and a threatening view of God; after Vatican II, the most persistent themes of sermons would be the love and mercy of God and the Eucharist as a sin-forgiving sacrament; in such circumstances, frequent confession would not be encouraged;

— many who approach it with the right spirit find that they are asking for bread and being given stones in return. In other words, their experience of the sacrament is unsatisfactory, so they stop going;

— since the 1960s there has been growing uncertainty amongst Catholics about what is sinful and what is not, especially in the area of sexual morality and the question of birth-control in particular;

— and, finally, there is a feeling that the sacrament cannot cope with the range of sinfulness in our world; it seemed to emphasise individual sins to the neglect of social sins like racism, the exploitation of the poor, and the arms race; also, 'my sins seem so trivial in comparison'.

To recover faith in the power of this sacrament, we need, first, to reflect on the gift of forgiveness and reconciliation that comes to us from the heart of God.

The Message of the Scriptures

A Sense of Liberation

The sacrament of confession, in the experience of many people, had belonged to a spirituality which reflected an obsession with sin and a sense of being overwhelmed by feelings of guilt. It encouraged within people a very poor image of themselves, with little experience of forgiveness and that sense of being accepted. People were well able to identify with St Peter's words: 'Depart from me, O Lord, for I am a sinful man'. They tended to regard God as a stern and stony God of endless demand and infinite reprisal, a God who condemns for repeated failure.

Confessional box

God never washes his hands of his people. It is such love which finds one of its most beautiful expressions in the prophecy of Hosea:

> *['My wife, Israel, has gone away with other lovers;] That is why I am going to lure her and lead her out into the wilderness and speak to her heart.'*
>
> (Hosea 2:14-16)

It is our task to respond when God cries out: 'Turn back and repent'; we must lament our infidelity; we must lament our ingratitude, our lack of love. Without such genuine sorrow and repentance there can be no forgiveness — a task made easier the more we appreciate how we are accepted by the love of God.

> **'Does a woman forget her baby at the breast, or fail to cherish the son of her womb? Yet, even if these forget, I will never forget you.'**
>
> *Isaiah 49:15*

It is such love that becomes flesh in the person of Jesus.

Jesus: the Friend of Sinners

Jesus was impatient with those who considered themselves sinless and thereby able to pass judgement on others:

> *'When the scribes of the Pharisee party saw him eating with sinners and tax collectors, they said to his disciples: "Why does he eat with tax collectors and sinners?" When Jesus heard this, he said to them: "It is not the healthy who need the doctor, but the sick. I did not come to call the virtuous but sinners".'*
>
> (Mark 2:16-17)

It is not in his contact with sinners that the crisis of the Gospel appears. With them, he can show himself simply as saviour, dissolving sin in his gracious approach. He was the friend of sinners and spoke to them with such sympathy it almost passes our understanding: Mary Magdalen, Zacchaeus, the woman taken in adultery, the publicans, the drop-outs. These people received nothing but kindness and compassion, releasing them from crippling physical and psychological burdens. And so, to Zacchaeus, 'one of the senior tax collectors and a wealthy man', Jesus says:

> *'Zacchaeus, come down. Hurry, because I must stay at your house today.'*
>
> (Luke 19:5)

Jesus does not judge him for his sinful actions, but enters into Zacchaeus' life in a way that he could feel

In the experience of Gerard Hughes, such a spirituality has caused mental breakdown or disillusionment, has fuelled anxiety neuroses, stunted moral development and has so filled some people with guilt that they now feel bad about being good, and all spontaneity, delight and joy has been banished from their lives (cf. *God of Surprises*, p.67). What a different God emerges from the pages of the Scriptures! A sense of liberation comes when its words are received in faith, words which constantly speak of a God who loves without measure, and loves to the end.

'Slow to anger, rich in graciousness' (Joel 2:13)

When we meet God, first of all, in the Old Testament, he is always crying to his people to turn back from other gods and return to him. He is our God. He chose us, we belong to him. He is desperately anxious for us to turn back to him. There is no one on earth so persevering as he is; he is repeatedly begging us to turn back to him. And so we read in Joel:

> *'"But now, now — it is Yahweh who speaks — come back to me with all your heart, fasting, weeping, mourning." Let your hearts be broken, not your garments torn, turn to Yahweh your God again, for he is all tenderness and compassion, slow to anger, rich in graciousness, and ready to relent.'*
>
> (Joel 2:12-13)

accepted, and invites him to the peace of reconciliation.

One of the best examples of Jesus' teaching is, of course, the parable of the prodigal son *(Luke 15:11-32)*. The sin of the prodigal son is not so much the riotous living as the turning away from his father and considering him dead by demanding his inheritance. The renewal of his relationship with his father begins at the point of despair where one flicker of faith is enough. He remembers the love he has shared with his father and acknowledges his guilt. On his return, he expects harshness and rejection, but instead he is treated like royalty and experiences extravagant forgiveness and, above all, reconciliation.

'Zacchaeus, come down.
Hurry, because I must stay at your house today.'

Jesus' Call to be a Community of Reconciliation

Throughout his ministry, therefore, Jesus talked passionately about forgiveness. This inevitably had tremendous consequences for his disciples. To the question posed by Peter: 'Lord, how often must I forgive my brother if he wrongs me? As often as seven times?' Jesus answered:

'Not seven, I tell you, but seventy-seven times.'
(Matthew 18:21-22)

In other words, forgiveness is not a matter of quantity but of quality. Forgiveness is not just an occasional act; it is a permanent attitude. It must, therefore, embrace not only friends but also enemies. No longer must it be 'an eye for an eye', 'a tooth for a tooth' but a forgiving love which loves until death. Such is the remarkable challenge of Jesus. In him we see the full potential of the human heart to forgive, especially when stretched out in agony on the cross:

'Father, forgive them; they do not know what they are doing.'
(Luke 23:34)

It was out of the experience of such forgiveness, on that first Easter morning, that the disciples received the mandate to forgive others. They could well have imagined that Jesus would want to make a totally fresh start after their loss of faith in the hour of crucifixion! Peter had denied all knowledge of Jesus and the rest had fled in disarray. They were men for whom God had no meaning and for whom death alone reigned *(Luke 24:20)*. The disciples had seen Jesus forgive others, but, surely, such forgiveness could not cover the enormity of their own sin. Like the prodigal son, they could only expect harshness and condemnation but, like him too, they received a marvellous surprise. They experienced for themselves the power of his mercy. With his gift of peace, their hearts were set free of guilt, fear and alienation, free to live again in the Spirit. It is no wonder that their primary mission was to offer the opportunity for others to be set free by the generous mercy of the Risen Lord:

> **'Peace be with you...Receive the Holy Spirit. For those whose sins you forgive, they are forgiven; for those whose sins you retain they are retained.'**
> *John 20:21-23*

Peace

Peace

Peace

How has the Church coped with this vital ministry of forgiveness and reconciliation?

Historical Development of the Sacrament of Penance

First Five Centuries: Canonical Penance

One of the most crucial questions discussed during the first three centuries of the Church was whether there could be any forgiveness of sins after baptism. Baptism was the sin-forgiving sacrament whereby we consider ourselves 'to be dead to sin but alive for God in Christ Jesus' *(Romans 6:11)*. Obviously, not everything was perfect and there would be tensions and jealousies amongst the new disciples. But this level of sinfulness would be overcome primarily in the celebration of the Eucharist, at the sign of peace and in reciting the Lord's Prayer.

It was soon recognised, however, that a 'second forgiveness' was needed. This gave rise to what is known as canonical penance.

▲ it was reserved for three serious sins: murder, adultery, and apostasy;

▲ the confessing of sins was not done in public, but the status of being a penitent most certainly was; penitents wore a distinctive dress of goat-skin (goats are the symbol of sinners) and they were excluded from the Eucharist;

▲ penances were severe: fasting; a period of exile in a monastery; no sexual relations, even in marriage;

▲ reconciliation was conducted by the bishop on Maundy Thursday and was allowed only once in a life-time.

Throughout this time, there was strong emphasis on the fact that peace and reconciliation with the Church was the sign of a person's reconciliation with God. The severity of canonical penance, however, soon proved unworkable. During a time of persecution, it was natural for the Church to stress the high and uncompromising demands of the Gospel ('once you put your hand to the plough' etc). But, in practice, people postponed reconciliation until their death-bed to ensure dying in a state of forgiveness and avoiding the long and hard punishments during their life-time. Pastoral circumstances demanded change.

6th - 12th Centuries: Tariffed Penance

Tariffed penance was so called because every sin earned a pre-arranged amount of penance, or a tariff. It began in Ireland and from there it quickly spread to the mainland of Europe. It developed through the monasteries where it was the custom for the monks to confess their faults to the abbott at least once a day. This practice gave basic shape to what became known as tariffed penance:

▲ it was essentially a private celebration involving a confession of faults (not necessarily serious) to an abbott or a priest appointed by him;

▲ it was repeatable and was available to everybody;

▲ most of the penances, though tough, could be performed at home without upsetting the penitent's normal way of life; books contained lists of sins with their appropriate penance (e.g. an impure thought calls for forty days' fast, while murder carries a ten year fast);

▲ the practice was closely associated with spiritual direction, providing a valuable means of moral education; it came to be seen, too, as a means of preparing for communion.

Although the Council of Toledo (589) spoke of this practice as being 'pernicious to the Catholic faith', one major advantage was that it enabled people to experience far more frequently the total availability of forgiveness within the Church. One serious drawback, however, was the practice of commutations whereby a short, sharp penance could be substituted for a longer and more wearisome one. As communion could only be received once the penance was completed, such commutations were often pastorally desirable. But there were inevitable abuses when penitents paid others to do penances for them; simony flourished and the wealthy were able to be reconciled with impunity. Sooner or later, the practice would have to be tidied up.

12th Century to the Present Day: Confession

During this period, we witness the emergence of the modern rite of penance which has lasted down to our own time. The main changes, which were gradually introduced, are as follows:

▲ the order of service was changed: the absolution now preceded the performing of the penance;

▲ what the penitent did by way of external penance was relatively light, eventually being reduced to a brief prayer or two;

▲ the difficult part of the sacrament was the act of confessing; it was only natural that the sacrament should now be called 'confession' rather than 'penance';

▲ stress was placed upon 'contrition' or a contrite heart on the part of the penitent as a most important element in this sacrament;

▲ the words of absolution were changed from 'May God forgive you' to 'I absolve you from your sins'.

Compared to earlier times, this form of the rite certainly acknowledged human weakness and the need for constant forgiveness. With the principal emphasis on confession, however, the priest assumed more the role of a judge, closely questioning penitents on the true extent of their sinfulness. For this reason, the sacrament quickly became a source of fear and alienation and, in the experience of many Catholics, has failed to symbolise the healing and forgiving love of Jesus. It was also a very private celebration and thus obscured the social nature of sin and that sense of being reconciled with the body of Christ. Through the work of the Second Vatican Council, the sacrament of confession has been revised and renamed the sacrament of reconciliation. The new name suggests emphasis on reconciling the sinner to God and the community, reflecting the attitude of Jesus. But first we will consider new ways of thinking about sin.

New Ways of thinking about Sin

Getting to the Root of the Matter!

When people ask 'what is sin today?', they often mean 'is this or that *activity* allowed, or is it still forbidden? And so, for example, people ask whether it is a sin to miss Mass on Sunday, or whether sex before marriage is a sin. These questions are important ones because behaviour is rightly regarded as the best index of character. We need only remember the words of Jesus: 'By their fruits you will know them'. Our behaviour reveals and shapes who we are: certain ways of acting can deform us, kill love in us and so destroy our relationship with God and with one another. Importance, therefore, must be given to our pattern of behaviour.

So often, though, we just concentrate on the sinful *actions* without paying heed to the sinful *attitude of heart* which gave rise to them. We concentrate on the symptoms rather than the root cause: the apathy, the cynicism, the closed-mindedness. If we wish to change our pattern of behaviour, therefore, like a good gardener or a good doctor we must get to the root of the matter by concentrating on underlying sinful attitudes. And so more fundamental questions might be: What am I proud about? What are my ambitions? What does sex mean for me? What am I lazy about?

© Carlos Reyes

A Sense of Alienation

The term 'alienation' describes well what is wrong with our human, sinful state. In our sin, we are *alienated from ourselves* because it destroys our self-respect. We are conscious of failing to live up to our full potential; we are alienated from that fullness of life to which we are called. We choose greed, envy, deceit, resentment, and injustice, instead of love, truth, kindness, honesty and compassion. St Paul speaks for all of us when he says:

> 'I cannot understand my own behaviour. I find myself doing the very things I hate...When I act against my will, then, it is not my true self doing it, but sin which lives in me.'
>
> *Romans 7:15,20*

We are *alienated, too, from one another*. Just as we accept the communion of saints so we need to recognise that we belong to the communion of sinners. It has been well said that every soul that rises above itself raises up the world. But the opposite is true as well: every soul that is closed-in and self-centred drags down the world. There is no such a thing as a purely private sin. Every sin, no matter how seemingly private and not harming anyone, makes us less a bearer of Christ for one another. As members of the body of Christ, we must recognise our responsibility in helping each other to overcome sin:

> *'Be at peace among yourselves. And this is what we ask you to do, brothers: warn the idlers, give courage to those who are apprehensive, care for the weak and be patient with everyone.'*
>
> (1 Thessalonians 5:14)

Finally, sin *alienates us from God himself*. He has created us in such a way that we can receive his love and share his love with one another. 'I will be your God, and you will be my people' runs like a refrain throughout the Scriptures, words which express the strength of God's commitment to us. Our very being is determined by what we may call the pull of love towards God and we can only find our true fulfilment in him. We are reminded of that famous saying of St Augustine:

> **'Thou hast created us for thyself and the heart is restless until it finds its resting-place in thee.'**

Sin strikes at the root of our relationship with God; far from being people called to love, through sin we become proud, vain, arrogant and self-centred; far from promoting unity and reconciliation, we are the bearers of division. Sin strikes at the heart of marriage and family life and spreads outwards to engulf whole nations.

A Helpful Analogy

It is helpful to liken our relationship with God to the relationship of marriage. In the context of married love, it is possible for quite serious things to go wrong without there being the intention to break the relationship. There can be misunderstandings, incidents of tension and insensitivity, of varying degrees of seriousness, which can damage the marriage relationship without putting it into jeopardy. On the other hand, a marriage relationship can so deteriorate over a period of time that the partners realise that the relationship is over.

In the same way, our commitment to Christ can withstand very serious failings. It is not easily broken. For this reason, theologians today speak of the various categories of sin as follows:

> **mortal sin** describes the state of the person who has abandoned his or her relationship with God. This may happen in a single moment; more frequently, however, it is the result of a slow process of moral and spiritual decline;
>
> **serious sins** refer to those moments in our life when we are inconsiderate, self-centred, and unfaithful, moments which seriously damage our relationship with God without breaking it. We might compare Peter's denial with Judas' betrayal;
>
> **venial sins** are those many daily faults with which we are all too familiar; left unattended they can gradually undermine our chosen commitment to Christ.

Such categories might not provide us with the clearest of guidelines for Christian living. They do, however, encourage us to set our sinfulness within the context of our relationship to Christ and the primacy of love that he sets before us. We are, then, not afraid to ask 'what do I really think is wrong with my life?' We do so in the confidence that no sin is too big for God's extravagant forgiveness. He loves us beyond measure and his one desire is that we receive what is best for us. It is in that spirit that we now turn to a consideration of the New Rite of Penance and Reconciliation.

The New Rite of Penance and Reconciliation

Reconciliation of Individual Penitents

This form of the new rite is equivalent to the old form of confession that we are accustomed to. But it includes a number of new features which are intended to breathe new life into the sacrament.

■ Prayer

Emphasis is placed, first of all, on the need for prayer:

> *'Priest and penitents should prepare themselves above all by prayer to celebrate the sacraments. The priest should call upon the Holy Spirit so that he may receive enlightenment and charity.'*
>
> (no.15)

Without this prayer, the priest will not be able to discern the deeper needs of the penitent; nor will the penitent be conscious of coming into the presence of a God who loves and whose one desire is to bring healing and forgiveness.

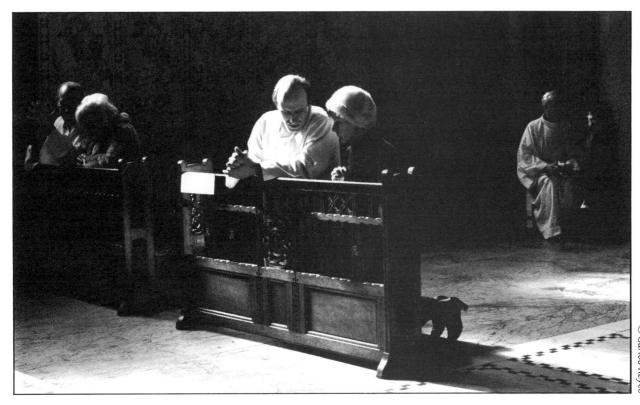

© Carlos Reyes

■ Welcome

The new rite encourages a far more relaxed and human relationship between priest and penitent. And so:

> 'When the penitent comes to confess his sins, the priest welcomes him warmly and greets him with kindness.'
>
> (no. 41)

The priest must establish the tone immediately by setting the penitent at ease and creating an atmosphere for a joint celebration of the Lord's forgiveness. Both priest and penitent make the sign of the cross together and then the penitent is encouraged to share a few details about his or her life. Such information provides an important setting for the confession of sin later on. In welcoming the penitent, the priest must reveal 'the heart of the Father and show the image of Christ the Good Shepherd' (no.10), as Jesus welcomed sinners into his company.

■ The Word of God

Priest and penitent, then, listen together to the word of God:

> 'Through the word of God Christians receive light to recognise their sins and are called to conversion and to confidence in God's mercy.'
>
> (no.17)

This is now an integral part of the new rite and must at least form part of the preparation for the sacrament. We are so accustomed to self-justification and self-protection. The word of God enables us to recognise

how weak and sinful we are; at the same time, it enables us to trust in God's unconditional love for us. Many marvellous texts are provided:

> 'Yahweh is tender and compassionate, slow to anger, most loving; his indignation does not last for ever... No less than the height of heaven over earth is the greatness of the love for those who fear him; he takes our sins farther away than the east is from the west.'
>
> Psalm 103:8,11-12

■ Confession

It is in the light of that word that the penitent is now encouraged to make his or her confession. No one finds this part of the sacrament easy! We do not know what to say in confession; we are dissatisfied with saying the same kind of thing every time we go; our pattern of confession can seem so childish. For these reasons, many have abandoned the practice of going to confession altogether. But still we feel a genuine need to acknowledge that we are sinners and, from our earlier considerations, we know the importance of getting to the root of the matter. And so, confession now frequently takes the form of a prayerful conversation between priest and penitent, perhaps focusing on a particular area of our life and its responsibilities, discerning our strengths and weaknesses, and gently opening our life to the healing power of the Holy Spirit. Such a confession needs time and is often, therefore, best conducted face to face without the pressure of many others waiting their turn. Confession by appointment, therefore, is not uncommon in many of our parishes. In all these matters, however, pastoral sensitivity is vitally important and no undue pressure must be placed on those who continue to be supported by a pattern of confession that has sustained them throughout their lives.

■ Penance, Act of Sorrow, Absolution

Following the confession, the priest suggests a particular penance. Traditionally, it has taken the form of saying a few prayers, representing a nominal gesture of good faith and reminding us that we need to renew ourselves and make up for any harm we may have caused by our sinfulness. The new rite recommends an act of penance more suited to our particular sinfulness and need for conversion: an act of kindness towards someone we have hurt. Penance is important because a habit of sin is not easily overcome and the consequences of our sinfulness can continue for others long after we have expressed our sorrow and received forgiveness.

The penitent now expresses sorrow. The best formula always comes from the heart, but the new rite suggests a number of formulas:

'Lord Jesus, you chose to be called the friend of sinners. By your saving death and resurrection free me from my sins. May your peace take root in my heart and bring forth a harvest of love, holiness, and truth.'

Without genuine sorrow and repentance there can be no forgiveness — it is required for the very possibility of the sacrament bearing fruit. 'Confession without change is a game.' (Thomas A. Harris, *I'm OK — You're OK*, p.222).

The most important task of the priest is to proclaim the prayer of forgiveness in the words of Absolution. As he does so, the new rite asks the priest to extend his hands over the penitent's head, recalling the many times that Jesus healed through touch. This prayer of forgiveness is a powerful reminder that the focus of the Christian message is not sin but the very opposite: the fact that God frees us from sin and constantly draws us into his company. The rite concludes with a short prayer of thanksgiving and dismissal such as:

'Go in peace and proclaim to the world the wonderful works of God who has brought you salvation.'

Reconciliation of several Penitents with Individual Confession

This form of the new rite provides a group celebration as a setting for individual confession. It follows the pattern of the first part of the Mass, with the penitential section following the homily. Its distinctive features need to be noted:

- the public examination of conscience can be a powerful means of helping people to form a genuinely Christian conscience, broadening their horizons and deepening their understanding of sin;

- it brings out the communal nature of sin and forgiveness: we pray for one another, witness each other's confession, and pledge our support for one another in our common search for a Christian way of life;

- its main drawback is that the time for actual confession must be kept brief.

© Catholic Pictorial

Peace and reconciliation between the Churches.

Peace and reconciliation within the Church

General Absolution

The third form of the sacrament of penance is similar to the one just outlined, but instead of individual confession, general absolution is given to all who wish it with a single, public formula. In addition to the normal conditions laid down for the reception of absolution, true repentance and satisfaction, there is one further condition: at the time of the general absolution, anyone in mortal sin must be resolved to confess those sins to a priest within a year.

The use of this rite, at the present time, is severely restricted, mainly to the kind of situation which often arises in mission territories where huge numbers of penitents cannot hope for individual confession from the few priests present. However, recent experience suggests that this rite should be made more widely available:

— it emphasises in a dramatic way the communal nature of forgiveness;

— it is truly a community celebration expressing the joy of sacramental reconciliation, especially for teenagers and lapsed Catholics who are genuinely afraid of approaching the priest in confession; perhaps in the same category are those committed Catholics who, for one reason or another, face a psychological block over the individual form of sacrament; general absolution provides a taste of the experience of the Prodigal Son;

— people feel more at ease going to personal confession after receiving general absolution; the two rites should be seen as complementary.

The Church is called to be a Community of Reconciliation

The sacrament points to an essential aspect of the nature of the Church itself: it must be recognised as a source of forgiveness and reconciliation. We must forgive as we have been forgiven, called to be ambassadors for Christ in the work of reconciliation.

This must be true, first and foremost, *within the Church* if we are to proclaim the Gospel effectively. We need to acknowledge the hurt that has caused so much bitterness in the lives of many of our own people. They include priests who have left the active ministry, the divorced and remarried, young people and women whose gifts have not been recognised, and many others who did not receive the helping hand when they needed it most. If we are truly the body of Christ we must constantly touch the lives of all these people with the generosity of Christ.

It is out of that kind of experience that we are called to proclaim the Gospel of forgiveness and reconciliation to a world devastated by sin and in so much need of conversion. There is the widespread violation of human rights with millions of people trapped in dire poverty, many innocent people captured and imprisoned for political dissent, and young children abused and murdered. There is the continuing sexual discrimination against women, which strikes at the heart of every aspect of human life. There is the senseless arms race whereby millions of pounds are spent year by year on weapons of war which can only kill and destroy, increasing the threat of a nuclear holocaust.

It is within such a world that the Church must stand for the possibility of forgiveness and reconciliation. Despite all the decay and suffering which seem to be constant factors of our world, our over-riding conviction must be that of St Paul:

> 'With God on our side who can be against us? Since God did not spare his own Son…we may be certain, after such a gift, that he will not refuse anything he can give…For I am certain of this: neither death nor life…nor any created thing can ever come between us and the love of God made visible in Christ Jesus our Lord.'
>
> *Romans 8:31-39*

Our circumstances demand a widespread change of heart, but we believe it to be possible because of the Spirit of God that has taken hold of our world.

Further Reading

Crichton, J.D. *The Ministry of Reconciliation*, Chapman, 1974

Fagan, Sean. *Has Sin Changed?* Michael Glazier, 1977

Hebblethwaite, M. *and* Donovan K. *The Theology of Penance*, Mercier Press, 1979

Hellwig, Monika K. *Sign of Reconciliation and Conversion*, Michael Glazier, 1984

Konstant, D. *and* Dodgson, D. *Forgiveness: the Sacrament of Penance Today*, Mayhew-McCrimmon, 1976

Matthews, Edward. *The Forgiveness of Sins*, Collins Liturgical, 1978

The Rite of Penance, Mayhew-McCrimmon, 1976

Sands, Ernest. *Penance and First Confession*, Unitape, 1983 [audiotape]

© Carlos Reyes

World Peace Assembly, Assisi, October 1986

ANOINTING OF THE SICK

Introduction

Traditionally, this sacrament has been the least attractive of all the sacraments. It was called 'Extreme Unction' — the Last Anointing — because it was associated almost exclusively with death. In the words of one writer, 'the anointed leap, so to speak, out of their death-beds straight into their thrones in heaven!' (Clifford Howell, *The Work of Our Redemption*, p.81). Although these words were intended to convey a sense of optimism in the face of death, the general atmosphere surrounding the sacrament was quite the opposite. Calling for a priest to perform the last rites was often a sign that all hope was lost, that there was no chance of recovery. For this reason, people postponed receiving the sacrament until the very last moment when further medical help was of no avail. It was affected by the same anxiety that surrounded death itself, 'celebrated' with black vestments and mournful chants heralding the last Judgement.

In more recent times, this sacrament has undergone a dramatic change of emphasis:

▲ no longer is it to be called 'Extreme Unction' or the Last Rites, but the 'Anointing of the Sick';

▲ the emphasis is now on the healing and raising up of the whole person and not simply on the forgiveness of sin in preparation for death;

▲ the sacrament is intended primarily for those who are seriously sick, including those preparing for major surgery, those suffering from serious mental stress, sick children of an age to understand, and those who are dying;

▲ ideally, the anointing should be a community celebration, drawing the sick person out of a sense of isolation.

Such changes are enabling this sacrament to be brought once more into the heart of the Church's sacramental life. No longer must we be afraid of it for it stands for the healing power of Jesus Christ reaching out to all those who are weighed down by sickness of mind and body. To appreciate the full richness of this sacrament, we must first reflect upon the concern Jesus himself showed for the sick in his life on earth.

The Healing Touch of Jesus

Jesus as Healer and Saviour

Jesus is our healer and saviour because he is first our companion and friend. He fully understands our situation because he became like us in all things but sin; he knows our weakness from personal experience. He experienced inner struggle, misunderstanding, rejection, betrayal, and the full horror of his own painful death on the cross. In his moment of darkness, Jesus shares with all men and women that sense of abandonment when life seems to be utterly without meaning.

Out of his own personal experience of weakness, Jesus was a source of life and healing for others. The basic experience of all those who came into contact with him and opened their hearts to him in expectation was one of well-being and liberation. Typical is the experience of the leper in Mark's Gospel:

'A leper came to him and pleaded on his knees: "If you want to", he said, "you can cure me". Feeling sorry for him, Jesus stretched out his hand and touched him. "Of course I want to!" he said. "Be cured!"'

(Mark 1:40-45)

Jesus was evidently 'moved with compassion' for all sick people and he healed them because he loved them and wanted to free them from their afflictions. Though constantly surrounded by crowds, Jesus always had time for the individual in need.

Jesus' work of healing formed an intrinsic part of his ministry:

'That evening they brought him many who were possessed by devils. He cast out the spirit with a word and cured all who were sick. This was to fulfil the prophecy of Isaiah: "He took our sicknesses away and carried our diseases for us!".'

(Matthew 8:16-17)

Jesus was uncompromising in his hostility to sickness in all its forms — whether it be bodily, spiritual or mental sickness. His concern is for the whole person and whatever it is that is holding that person back from a wholesome relation with God and the community. Jesus warns us against attributing sickness to personal sinfulness in every case *(John 9:2-3)*, but he does teach us that unforgiven sin is one of the chief sources of unhappiness and many kinds of sickness *(Mark 2:5)*. In bringing healing into people's lives, Jesus was always concerned to go to the heart of the matter:

'Seeing their faith, Jesus said to the paralytic, "My child, your sins are forgiven".'

(Mark 2:5)

Jesus cures the leper

Jesus entrusts Healing Power to his Disciples

Jesus was just as eager for his disciples to heal the sick and so his last recorded words in Mark are as follows:

'These are the signs that will be associated with believers...they will lay their hands on the sick, who will recover.'

(Mark 16:17-18)

And again in St John's Gospel:

'I tell you most solemnly, whoever believes in me will perform the same works as I do myself; he will perform even greater works, because I am going to the Father. Whatever you ask for in my name I will do, so that the Father may be glorified in the Son. If you ask for anything in my name, I will do it.'

(John 14:12-14)

The Church, therefore, is called to be a healing Church simply because it is the Church of Jesus Christ commissioned to continue his ministry. A key text in this context, of course, is the well-known passage from the Letter of St James, the only explicit reference in the New Testament to what we have since come to call 'the anointing of the sick':

> **'If one of you is ill, he should send for the elders of the church, and they must anoint him with oil in the name of the Lord and pray over him. The prayer of faith will save the sick man and the Lord will raise him up again; and if he has committed any sins, he will be forgiven.'**
>
> *James 5:14-15*

St James is concerned to impress on his readers that God truly hears the prayer of whoever places his trust in him. In particular, the poor and the suffering can always have hope in the goodness and faithfulness of God. In this case, St James tells us, 'the prayer of faith will save the sick man'. The most obvious meaning of these words would seem to be that the sick man will receive all that he needs at the time from a faithful God who cares for the whole person. Notice, too, that St James stresses the power of the prayer of faith of the gathered community. How has the Church coped with this ministry over the centuries?

The Sacrament of Anointing within Christian Tradition

Until 750 (the medicinal period)

There were no rituals during this time; it was more a case of charismatic improvisation. The people themselves bought their own oil and brought it to the Church so that it could receive the bishop's blessing during the eucharistic celebration. The presiding bishop prayed that 'it may give strength to all who taste it and strength to all who use it'. Afterwards, people would take the blessed oil to their homes for use in case of sickness within their families. Emphasis was placed primarily on bodily healing and so this period is referred to as 'the medicinal period'; there was no mention of the condition that a person should be in danger of death. The full effects of this anointing with oil are well expressed in a beautiful prayer from fourth century Egypt:

> 'Through the power of Christ's death and resurrection may the oil drive away all illness and infirmity... bring to the sick your good favour and the forgiveness of sins, that it be for them a life-giving remedy, that it bring them health and wholeness of body, soul and spirit, and perfect vigour.'

(From the Prayer Book of Bishop Serapion, cited by C. Walsh in *Christian Ministry to the Sick*, Chapman, 1986.)

From 800 - 1150 (connection with penance)

Within a very short period of time, anointing of the sick as an informal practice carried out by lay people within their own homes virtually disappeared. The collapse of the Roman Empire and the danger posed by all manner of superstitions and pagan practices demanded the need for reform. It was now insisted that priests administer the sacrament of anointing in the context of their own ministry to the sick and the dying. In practice, their ministry was primarily concerned with the dying and so anointing came to form a continuous rite with penance and viaticum of the dying. The formula used in anointing the five senses was as follows:

> 'Through this holy anointing (and God's blessing) may the Lord forgive you whatever sins you have committed by the sense of...'

Physical healing was no longer expected; indeed, if the patient should recover, he was considered to be living on borrowed time, 'since once anointed he is dead to the world'! The sacrament was now referred to as 'Extreme Unction' — a consecration for death.

From 1150 - 1550 (the sacrament of the dying)

The Great Scholastics of the thirteenth and fourteenth centuries translated the practice of their day into dogmatic principles. Now, danger of death was a condition for receiving the sacrament and it could only be received once. And so, St Thomas Aquinas could describe it as

> 'the last remedy the Church can offer and all but immediately disposes a person for glory. This is why it is only administered to those who are dying.'
> (Cited by C. Walsh, *op cit*)

The effect of the sacrament is essentially the forgiveness of sins in preparation for entry into eternal life.

From the Council of Trent until the Present Time

Surprisingly, the Council of Trent did not canonise this understanding of the sacrament of anointing. It spoke of the recipients of the sacrament as 'the sick, especially those who are so dangerously ill that they seem to be at the point of leaving this life'. The Holy Spirit, it said, was the gift of anointing which could bring about bodily healing when it is of help for salvation. The Council of Trent, therefore, tried to overcome the narrow discipline canonised by the Great Scholastics. But prevailing attitudes were too deeply entrenched. Despite an appeal by Pope Benedict XIV in 1753 to return to the ancient custom of the Church, the sacrament continued to be understood as 'Extreme Unction' — exclusively for the dying.

As we have seen, it wasn't until the Second Vatican Council that Pope Benedict XIV's appeal was heeded, when it was affirmed that this sacrament is more properly called 'anointing of the sick', its primary purpose being:

> 'to give the grace of the Holy Spirit to those who are sick: by this grace the whole person is helped and saved, sustained by trust in God, and strengthened against the temptations of the Evil One and against anxiety over death.'

Before examining the New Rite of Pastoral Care of the Sick in more detail, we must first reflect upon the experience of sickness itself.

The Experience of Sickness

A Sense of Alienation

In order to respond fully to the needs of a sick person, it is important that we understand what he/she feels — psychologically, spiritually, emotionally, as well as physically. Sickness is a moment filled not only with physical pain and suffering but also with a sense of alienation and isolation, fear and uncertainty. One aspect of this alienation is that a sick person becomes acutely aware of his own body — its pain, its numbness, its nausea. Alienation and isolation are further experienced at the level of being withdrawn from normal everyday life. This means being confined to bed, either at home or in hospital, isolated from all those activities which make life worth living.

Sickness involves a marginal existence which seems only to speak of exclusion from the life that matters. The world of the sick person shrinks to the size of the bedroom and challenges all the basic assumptions we take so much for granted. In such circumstances, a sick person feels that he or she has nothing to contribute except to remain in a state of total helplessness. And the sense of alienation is completed by the feeling of abandonment by God himself. Prayer becomes impossible and there is nothing left but the feeling of devastation: 'Why should this happen to me? I've tried to be a good person. I have a wife and young children who need me. I don't deserve this. Why should God make me suffer like this?'

© Michael Silver

Response to Sickness

Why one person gets sick and another does not we shall never know. What really matters is the response to the sickness that comes our way. A sense of guilt often haunts the sick. And this for a number of reasons: resentment and bitterness; personal indulgence in drinking, smoking, over-eating, etc; the burden that sickness places on family and friends; and the feeling that sickness is a punishment from God. It is natural that a first reaction should be one of anger and denial because it takes time to come to terms with serious sickness. It is an instinctive reaction to life's seeming unfairness but it must not give way to morbid self-pity. Family and friends must provide vital support and understanding if the one who is sick is to react positively to his or her suffering and to see it not as waste nor as punishment but as opportunity.

Pastoral Care of the Sick and the Dying

The New Ritual, published in Great Britain in 1983, is concerned with the rite of anointing and the rite of viaticum. It contains material, therefore, for ministry both to the sick and the dying and makes clear that communion and anointing are the fundamental sacraments for the sick and that viaticum is the sacrament for the dying. Valuable pastoral guidelines are provided in each section, and alternative ways of celebrating the sacraments are suggested, depending on practical circumstances and the degree of emergency. Throughout the new rite, it is evident that the Church's primary concern is to reduce the sense of alienation and isolation to a minimum and to help the sick and the dying to experience the compassion of Christ. Such concern, however, does not begin in the moment of sickness itself.

Importance of our Whole Experience of Life

Facing up to sickness and death demands an experience of support and encouragement throughout the whole course of our lives:

— We need to assure one another that our God is a God who is with us in every moment, a God who is always on the side of the victim, sharing that sense of being abandoned in the midst of pain and suffering. Being in communion within the Church means that no one need feel alone or isolated.

— We need to provide a strong source of support for the many 'little deaths' that inevitably come our way: a change of job or retirement; the experience of divorce or redundancy; an inability to bear children; miscarriages or the birth of a handicapped child. Our sensitivity to these moments helps to build up that essential atmosphere of trust if we are to let go successfully.

— We are helped to face up to our own death by experiencing the reaction of the community to the deaths of others. A community that is not afraid to gather round its dying and to be fully present to the bereaved, helping them to rebuild their lives, is by that very fact building up the faith and hope of the community and providing an almost tangible presence of the caring and compassionate God.

— Finally, we must keep alive a strong faith in the communion of saints. The mourner's real concern is communion with those who have died and this mystery of our faith impresses on us that fellowship with our loved ones does not cease with death. Through prayer in Christ we are able to remain forever in communion with those who have gone before us in faith.

Visiting the Sick

Two chapters of *Pastoral Care of the Sick* are devoted to visiting the sick: one deals with sick adults, the other with sick children. The General Introduction describes this ministry in the following terms:

> 'Kindness shown towards the sick
> and works of charity and mutual help
> for the relief of every kind of human want
> are held in special honour...
> and may be considered a sharing
> in Christ's healing ministry.'
>
> *nos. 32-33*

As we have seen, sickness brings with it a sense of loneliness and isolation and therefore the intention of such visits is to reassure the sick person that he or she is not forgotten; the community is concerned and is anxious for him or her to recover.

The responsibility for such an important ministry lies not simply with the priest but with the whole Christian community; lay people must be recognised as representing the whole community, revealing the Lord who is always at our side. This point, too, receives considerable emphasis within the new rite:

© Carlos Reyes

> 'This ministry is the common responsibility
> of all Christians,
> who should visit the sick,
> remember them in prayer,
> and celebrate the sacraments with them.
> The family and friends of the sick,
> doctors and others who care for them,
> and priests with pastoral responsibilities
> have a particular share
> in the ministry of comfort.
> Through words of encouragement and faith
> they can help the sick
> to unite themselves with the sufferings
> of Christ for the good of God's people.'

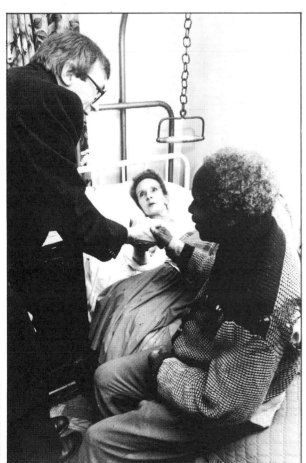
© Catholic Pictorial

God is love

© Carlos Reyes

Lourdes

Healing through Prayer

A visit to the sick person should include a time of prayer together. We remember the promise of Jesus that when we ask in faith, in his name, then he will answer our prayer. There is no special technique; the only requirement is that the prayer we say comes from a heart filled with faith and love:

> 'Have faith in God. I tell you solemnly, if anyone says to this mountain, "Get up and throw yourself into the sea", with no hesitation in his heart but believing that what he says will happen, it will be done for him. I tell you, therefore: everything you ask and pray for, believe that you have it already, and it will be yours.'
>
> *Mark 11:21-25*

Such prayer will inevitably be made with expectant faith, believing that the Lord wants to, can, and will help in this particular situation here and now. So often, our prayer is wholly directed towards asking God that the sick person might be able to bear his or her sufferings with patience. This is important but we must not be blind to the possibilities of healing that the Lord can bring about in response to prayer:

— there is the possibility of *physical healing* through prayer which, in view of the teaching of the New Testament, we must not minimise. Such healing has traditionally been associated with special people and special places such as Lourdes. We need to expect much more in the way of healing of sickness through prayer within our ordinary local communities;

— but we should never pray for healing of the body without praying for *healing of the spirit and mind*. It is commonly appreciated today that many people become sick because they nourish grudges and bitterness in their hearts. Failure to love and forgive, bitterness, resentment, jealousy, envy etc are not just spiritual sicknesses; they are frequently the cause of many sicknesses of a psychosomatic nature such as stress, heart attacks and cancer.

The fact that sometimes even persistent prayers for healing are not answered by the kind of healing we seek does not mean, necessarily, that those prayers are without sufficient faith. As soon as we pray at all, we enter the realm of the mystery of God's love and power, and we cannot have all the answers. We can only depend on God's goodness and accept reverently his answers to our prayers in whatever form he chooses it to take.

Healing through Worship

The most important sacrament of healing is undoubtedly the Eucharist, as we find expressed in so many of its prayers:

'You were sent to heal the contrite, Lord have mercy...'; 'Take this, all of you, and drink from it: this is the cup of my blood, the blood of the new and everlasting covenant. It will be shed for you and for all people so that sins may be forgiven. Do this in memory of me'; 'Lord, I am not worthy to receive you, but only say the word and I shall be healed.'

■ Communion of the Sick

Communion of the sick, therefore, is a vital means of drawing sick people out of their isolation and enabling them to feel part of the parish community, especially on Sunday. This is made possible today because of the valuable introduction of special ministers of communion, ordinary men and women chosen from their local community and commissioned by the bishop to share in the ministry of distributing communion. It is a ministry that has brought tremendous joy to so many sick people and their families as they are given access to the Eucharist frequently and made to feel at home within the body of Christ. As so many people are now involved in this ministry, visits to the sick are becoming less rushed, providing time for the short service to be conducted in an unhurried way, and time, too, for a chat and a cup of tea, gradually establishing that necessary personal relationship which this ministry demands.

■ Sacrament of Anointing

The sacrament most associated with the sick, of course, is the sacrament of anointing. Since it is now firmly established as a sacrament for the sick, the sick person will find reassurance from the prayers of the new rite:

'Lord Jesus Christ, our Redeemer, by the power of the Holy Spirit, ease the sufferings of our sick brother (sister), and make him well again in mind and body. In your loving kindness forgive his sins and grant him full health so that he may be restored to your service.'

(Prayer after the Anointing)

© Carlos Reyes

There is no mention of death; the whole thrust of the new rite is that the sick person should struggle against the sickness and desire the blessing of good health once again. In addition to the prayer of the community for the sick person, the other two elements of the rite are the laying-on of hands and the anointing of the sick person, which, at the moment, can only be carried out by the priest. The sacrament is administered by anointing the sick on the forehead and hands with blessed oil as the priest prays that the Lord will heal the sick person and extend his saving grace:

> '*Through this holy anointing may the Lord in his love and mercy help you with the grace of the Holy Spirit. Amen.*
> *May the Lord who frees you from sin save you and raise you up.*'

Celebrations of the sacrament of anointing the sick generally take place within the home or in the hospital with just a small circle of family and friends, and, if possible, within Mass. But what is frequently recommended today is that such celebrations take place publicly within the parish and in other large gatherings, such as on Lourdes' pilgrimages. A remarkable example of such a celebration took place at St George's Cathedral, Southwark on 28 May 1982 during the visit of John Paul II to Britain. It has been described as one of the most moving and emotional acts of his British tour and will always be remembered for those frequently quoted words from his sermon:

> '**Do not neglect your sick and elderly. Do not turn away from the handicapped and the dying. Do not push them to the margins of society. For if you do, you will fail to understand that they represent an important truth...that weakness is a creative part of human living.**'

Such an occasion must surely be a regular feature of every parish or deanery, providing a marvellous opportunity for a dramatic, joyful celebration of the love and compassion of Christ. First of all, it enables the housebound to meet old friends and relax in a social atmosphere and, above all, to feel part of the parish community; and secondly, it reminds the rest of the community that the sick are their brothers and sisters, who need their prayers and loving concern. It also enables so many of the community to become involved in its preparation: transport, provision of tea, and the liturgy itself. The healing powers of the sacrament stretch far beyond those specifically brought to the Church to receive the anointing. But what is the purpose of all this healing?

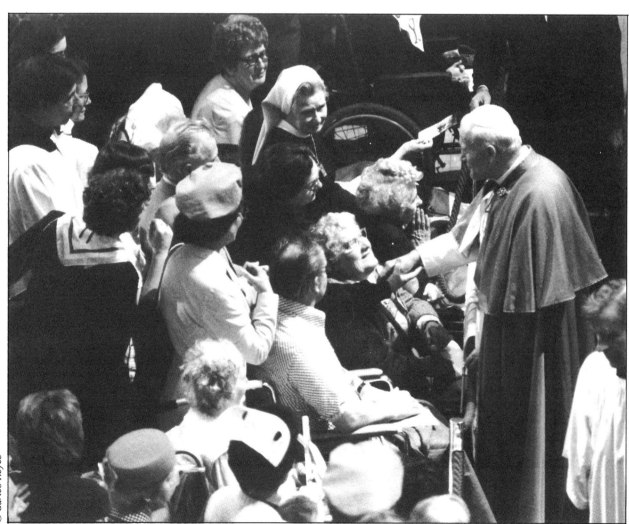

© Carlos Reyes

John Paul II at St George's Cathedral, May 1982

© Catholic Pictorial

'Mentally handicapped people are the prophets of an age.'

Vocation of the Sick and the Dying

In Weakness we are Strong

In their sickness, and in all they have to endure by way of suffering, the sick have so much to teach us. They teach us, first of all, that there is much more to life than good looks, plenty of money, getting a good job, and affording a holiday. They may seem so helpless and yet they can lead us to see what is important in life on this earth and essential for life eternal. Their courage, their trust, their very helplessness, teach us the kind of values that must lie at the heart of human relationships. They call for a profound reverence for one another as individuals, a recognition of our fundamental dependence on one another and, above all, a spirit of confidence that we can overcome even the most cruel misfortunes.

And so, for example, Nouwen has written: 'Our first and most important task is to help the elderly become our teachers again and to restore the broken connections among the generations.' (*Ageing*, p.17). They have so much to teach us: the way God remains faithful to those who trust him; the meaning and purpose of life in the midst of weakness, dependence, powerlessness, and in the face of death; the need to face up to change and the danger of making idols of particular ways, institutions, and traditions; and the importance of prayer. The elderly have a most valuable ministry within our local parishes.

So, too, have mentally handicapped people. Bishop Daly of Derry has spoken of them in the following terms:

'Mentally handicapped people are the prophets of an age, because they tell us about the futility of wealth in a world where we are only refugees running from one problem to another; they trust us so absolutely and demonstrate the value of trust in a world where the word has lost its meaning.'

We need to discover ways whereby such essential gifts, which find expression in and through their disability, can become central to the ministry of the Church.

'The Dying are our Teachers'

The phrase belongs to Elizabeth Kubler Ross who has done so much in recent years to liberate people from the fear of dying by stressing the need to create an atmosphere of trust and openness. Ninety-nine per cent of those dying know intuitively the truth of their condition but they are afraid to share such knowledge because they detect fear and anxiety in those around them. The latter in the meantime ask everyone to make sure that the dying person is not allowed to guess the seriousness of his condition, 'because it would be too painful for him'. There often appears to be a conspiracy of silence. Within a relationship of trust, however, a dying person is able to share the dawning realisation of what is happening to his body and spirit and his reaction to it. Kubler Ross has taught us that by patiently listening to the dying we come to understand the basic emotions involved in coming to terms with personal death:

denial: a healthy reaction because it takes time to come to terms with death and we must give them that time;

anger: again, a natural reaction; blame is attached to staff, doctors, family, God — no one can do anything right; a particularly difficult emotional time for the family; there is need for understanding and an active assurance of acceptance and support, in this way providing an escape valve for the anger;

bargaining: a sign of a living person hanging on to life: 'if I tried this medicine, this doctor, etc;

despair: the final realisation 'it is me'; closeness through touch and comfortable silence is so vital if a dying person is to be drawn out of despair;

acceptance: the beginning of a new stage of life which grasps the importance of the present moment; the true values in life, in the most ordinary things, in relationships, are brought into sharper focus; there comes, too, a sense of peace and a renewed trust in the presence of God.

It is the responsibility of the whole Christian community to gather round its dying and their family and friends, providing an almost tangible presence of the caring, compassionate God. This is done best simply by being there; words are so often inadequate when what is needed is that closeness through touch and comfortable silence referred to earlier. Prayer, of course, is of vital importance at this time, expressing our faith in the promises of Jesus that the destiny of our life is nothing less than the merciful, eternal call of the love of God. And the sacramental love of Jesus, too, extends to this moment. The sacrament intended for this stage of life is a special form of Communion of the sick, called **Viaticum**. This is the real sacrament of the dying and is intended as food for the journey from this life to the next. It is well to remember that it can be given under the form of wine only when swallowing proves difficult.

'The celebration of the Eucharist as viaticum, food for the passage through death to eternal life, is the sacrament proper to the dying Christian. It is the completion and crown of the Christian life on this earth, signifying that the Christian follows the Lord to eternal glory and the banquet of the heavenly kingdom. The sacrament of the anointing of the sick should be celebrated at the beginning of a serious illness. Viaticum, celebrated when death is close, will then be better understood as the last sacrament of Christian life.'
(Pastoral Care of the Sick, 175)

Once a loved one has died, the Christian community must gather round those who are bereaved, helping them to rebuild their lives. Bereavement is the price we pay for loving and there is nothing we can say that will take away the pain. Instead, we can help by sharing the experience and allowing the bereaved person to grieve openly and talk about the pain. A remarkable testimony to the experience of bereavement has recently been given by Margaret Calderbank in a book entitled *One of Us is Missing*. She tells the story of the death of her young son on a football field and relives, in a most vivid way, this time of sadness, showing how faith and love can overcome even the greatest tragedy. She concludes:

'I was so heartbroken, I could not find consolation or reasoning in anything, but then gradually the realisation that Christ loved me became crystal clear. He had chosen Francis for himself, He loved him, and through him, had shown His love for me also.

He placed His cross upon my shoulders. I felt its weight physically. No amount of aspirin relieved the pain, and then he removed it when it became too heavy, and replaced it with love, and compassion, wisdom and joy.'

Further Reading

Coyle, Tom (ed.). *Christian Ministry to the Sick*, Chapman, 1986

Haring, Bernard. *Healing and Revealing*, St Paul Publications, 1984

Kushner, Harold S. *When Bad Things Happen to Good People*, Avon Books, 1983

McManus, Jim. *The Healing Power of the Sacraments*, Redemptorist Publications, 1984

Pastoral Care of the Sick: Rites of Anointing and Viaticum, Chapman, 1983

Sands, Ernest. *Anointing of the Sick*, Unitape, 1982 [audiotape]

Note: Some material in this chapter is dealt with at greater length by the author in chapter five (Theology of Sickness) of *Christian Ministry to the Sick*, Chapman, 1986.

MARRIAGE

Marriage: never more popular, never more risky

Marriage, today, is as popular as ever. Ninety per cent of men and women will have been married by the age of forty and, despite all the publicity and pressures to the contrary, there is a strong feeling that marriage should be for ever. Such a feeling is so evident amongst those who attend a wedding. It is an occasion of tremendous joy when there is so much evidence of goodness amongst people firmly believing in the faithfulness of human love. Everyone, young and old alike, acknowledges that this day is unique in the lives of a couple who decide to share their future life together. It involves a great act of faith and represents one of the greatest compliments one human being can pay to another.

The challenge of such an act of faith is by no means an impossible ideal. Countless married Christians have lived, and live today, quiet lives of great dedication, gradually deepening their commitment and love. Because of their faith in Jesus, they truly believe in the capacity of the human heart to love to the end. Unfortunately, none have been canonised as examples of married holiness!

Yet we know that this is not the whole story. In recent years, there has been such a dramatic increase in the number of divorces that now one in three or four marriages are likely to break down. Underlying these figures is a picture of considerable personal suffering, loneliness and daily tension, especially when we remember the number of children involved. It is estimated that something like 500,000 people in Great Britain are affected each year by the tragedy of marriage breakdown.

When reflecting on the reasons for these alarming figures, we need to bear in mind some of the changes and tensions which have profoundly affected the experience of family life today:

- marriages which survive are lasting much longer: golden anniversaries are not uncommon;

- women are experiencing more freedom in marriage and are desiring equality in the marriage relationship;

- the strain of economic factors often means that both husband and wife have to work; poor housing and unemployment bring added strains;

- another factor is the isolation of the family unit away from the support of parents, old friends and neighbours;

- the need for adaptation from first love through to old age;

- instability caused by easy divorce laws.

How can we continue to uphold the vision of life-long fidelity in marriage in the midst of such experiences? How can we enable people who have suffered the pain of marriage breakdown to experience the forgiveness, mercy and compassion of God?

Biblical Roots of Marriage

'Male and female He created them' (Genesis 1:27)

The basic goodness of marriage and the fundamental equality of the sexes is presented in the opening chapters of Genesis:

> 'God created man in the image of himself, in the image of God he created him, male and female he created them.'
>
> *Genesis 1:27*

It took a little while, however, before this remarkable teaching was proposed as the moral ideal in marriage. Solomon, for example, and other kings had many wives and concubines; and divorce was an accepted way of ending an unhappy marriage. A common reason is simply stated by Deuteronomy:

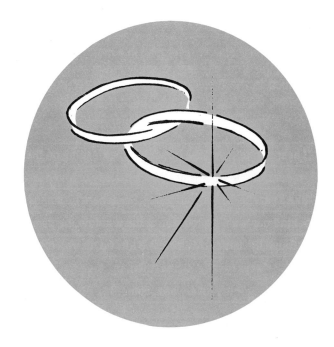

'She has not pleased him and he has found some impropriety of which to accuse her; so he has made out a writ of divorce for her and handed it to her and then dismissed her from his house.'

(Deuteronomy 24:1)

In the midst of all of this, however, there was genuine concern expressed for the need to support husband and wife in their commitment to one another. And so, for example, the following provisions are made for the newly-married man:

'If a man is newly married, he shall not join the army nor is he to be pestered at home; he shall be left at home free of all obligations for one year to bring joy to the wife he has taken.'

(Deuteronomy 24:5)

Marriage as Mirror of God's Covenant

At the heart of the Old Testament is the story of God's love for his people, of the Covenant he made with them. They broke the Covenant many times, but God never revoked it. However fickle and unreliable they were in loving God, he was always steadfast and faithful. The prophet Hosea was the one who represented this Covenant relationship of God with his people as a marriage. In the story, the broken-hearted prophet Hosea is told by God to forgive his wife — quite a break with even the strictest tradition allowing divorce:

'That is why I am going to lure her and lead her out into the wilderness and speak to her heart... There she will respond to me as she did when she was young, as she did when she came out of the land of Egypt.'

(Hosea 2:15-16)

The figure of Hosea is a symbol of the Covenant love of God for his people; that radically faithful, steadfast and forgiving love God is always pouring out on his chosen ones.

This same theme is developed in a most remarkable way in the Song of Songs, a collection of love poems included in the Bible as a picture of the relationship between God and his people. The poet is familiar with sexual experience and quite obviously enjoys it:

'I hear my Beloved. See how he comes leaping on the mountains, bounding over the hills. My beloved is like a gazelle, like a young stag. See where he stands behind our wall. He looks in at the window, he peers through the lattice. My Beloved lifts up his voice, he says to me, "Come, then, my love, my lovely one, come."'

Song of Songs 2:8-10

Through the insight of the prophets, the people of the Old Testament gradually came to see the union in love between husband and wife as the mirror of God's faithfulness towards them. It finds beautiful expression in the final words of Tobias' prayer on his wedding night:

'And so I do not take my sister for any lustful motive; I do it in singleness of heart. Be kind enough to have pity on her and on me and bring us to old age together.'

(Tobit 8:9)

The Teaching of Jesus on Marriage

The explicit teaching of Jesus on this question must be set within the context of the self-giving love of Jesus and the kind of love he asks of his disciples. We see in Jesus the capacity of the human heart to love, to forgive, to suffer and to heal; and he calls his disciples to love in the same totally selfless way, firmly believing that nothing is beyond forgiveness and that love, like hope, springs eternal. Only a couple of examples of this kind of teaching are necessary:

'Anyone who wants to save his life will lose it; but anyone who loses his life for my sake will find it.'
(Matthew 16:25)

'This poor widow has put more in than all who have contributed...for they have all put in money they had over, but she from the little she had has put in everything she possessed.'

(Mark 12:43-44)

It should be no surprise, therefore, that Jesus speaks in the same terms of lasting fidelity in marriage:

'From the beginning of creation God made them male and female. This is why a man must leave father and mother, and the two become one body. They are no longer two, therefore, but one body. So then, what God has united, man must not divide.'

(Mark 10:6-9)

These words represent the original teaching of Jesus on the subject of divorce: the permanence of marriage belongs to the intention of his Father in the moment of creation and, therefore, divorce is against the will of God. In Matthew's Gospel, however, we have the famous phrase: 'except for the case of fornication' *(Matthew 5:32; 19:9)*, which seems to suggest an exception to Jesus' teaching. It is difficult to know exactly what this phrase means but it does suggest that from earliest times the Christian community has struggled with the challenge of living up to the high ideals of Jesus on the permanence of marriage. This tension is evident throughout the Scriptures as we recall the numerous words of forgiveness and reconciliation which must apply to marriage in a particular way.

The Teaching of St Paul

In St Paul's letters, there are many references to marriage, which are obviously conditioned by the customs of his time, and by the expectation that the Lord's second coming would happen quite soon. Although he himself preferred to remain single, and some of his comments about women would be quite out of place today, many of his ideas about marriage and family life were centuries ahead of his time, and remain as ideals for us today. And so he writes:

> *'The husband must give his wife what she has the right to expect, and so too the wife to the husband. The wife has no rights over her own body; it is the husband who has them. In the same way, the husband has no rights over his body; the wife has them.'*
>
> (1 Corinthians 7:3-4)

Such love between husband and wife, perhaps, finds its most moving expression in the letter to the Ephesians:

> **'Give way to one another in obedience to Christ. Wives should regard their husbands as they regard the Lord...Husbands should love their wives just as Christ loved the Church and sacrificed himself for her to make her holy...In the same way husbands must love their wives as they love their own bodies.'**
>
> *Ephesians 5:21-28*

The love expected from both husband and wife is equally demanding and is only possible on the basis of their marriage being founded 'in the Lord'. Both are called upon to reflect in their love the self-sacrificing attitude of Christ; indeed, it is in their love for one another that husband and wife experience the presence of the risen Christ. The qualities of such love are well known to us:

> *'Love is always patient and kind; it is never jealous; love is never boastful or conceited; it is never rude or selfish; it does not take offence, and is not resentful. Love takes no pleasure in other people's sins but delights in the truth; it is always ready to excuse, to trust, to hope, and to endure whatever comes. Love does not come to an end.'*
>
> (1 Corinthians 13:4-7)

We now turn to a consideration of the Church's developing understanding of Christian marriage. The words of Jesus provided a tremendous challenge and gradually led the Church to give special care to those who wished to remain faithful to one another in married love.

An Understanding of Marriage within Christian Tradition

Gradual Unfolding of the Church's Responsibilities

■ Beginnings of Pastoral Care

During the first three centuries of Christianity, Christian marriages were performed no differently from any other marriages. Christians just followed the local custom. In their hearts, however, they would know that, because of their faith in Christ, their commitment was for life and must reflect the faithful love of God for his people. For this reason, as early as AD 107, Ignatius advised that those getting married should do so with the advice of their bishop; and about a hundred years later, Tertullian describes the happiness of a marriage which the Church supports with her blessing. In these early days, therefore, the Church was primarily concerned with helping Christians to recognise what it meant to be married 'in the Lord'. Indeed so strong was the emphasis placed upon their baptismal commitment that marrying a pagan was forbidden.

■ Emergence of Church Celebration

From the fourth century onwards, there was a gradual development of Church blessings and prayers which were offered in addition to the civil procedures. This was more pronounced within the East where the clergy took quite an active role, joining the couple in marriage and blessing the union. In Rome, at this time, the marriage ceremony was followed by the celebration of the Eucharist and a special blessing. This marked the beginning of our nuptial Mass and was a powerful expression of the Church's desire to help newly-married couples to remain faithful in their love for each other.

■ The Church assumes Full Responsibility

With the decline of civil authority, due to the barbarian invasions, during the ninth century the Church began to assume full jurisdiction over all marriages. This meant not only performing the actual wedding ceremony, but also deciding who was able to get married. One particular problem concerned the vast number of secret marriages. Until now, the validity of marriage only depended on the mutual consent of two baptised Christians. Such a marriage was now forbidden to protect people who might be forced or deceived into marrying in private. The process demanded many detailed laws governing a valid marriage and they are with us to this day. The most significant development in this connection is the famous decision made by the Council of Trent in 1563: from now on all Catholic marriages, to be valid, must take place before a priest and two witnesses. This rule was not universally applied but it did have the effect of placing marriage firmly in the public sphere.

The Church's Discovery of Marriage as Sacrament

■ Influence of St Augustine

St Augustine was the only one of the Fathers of the Church to write extensively about sex and marriage. Throughout his writings he struggled between his desire to emphasise the goodness of marriage, on the one hand, and his own deeply ingrained feeling that sex is evil and degrading, on the other. Nevertheless, it was largely due to his influence that the Church proclaimed the goodness and holiness of marriage. He identified what he referred to as the three 'goods' of marriage:

— the only fully legitimate reason for having sexual relations is to produce children;

— it is a concession to the desires of the flesh and fosters faithfulness between a man and a woman;

— it is a sacred sign of the union between Christ and his Church and therefore, 'the marriage bond is only dissolved by the death of one of the partners.' *(On the Good of Marriage, 24).*

■ The Teaching of St Thomas Aquinas

St Thomas Aquinas was inevitably influenced by St Augustine's view that the desire for children was the only justification for sexual intercourse. Nevertheless, he does present a very positive view of marriage which regards married love as the greatest possible human love:

— the shame surrounding sex is not because sexual intercourse itself is sinful; it is because of a disorder within us resulting from original sin;

— the grace of marriage brings holiness and the capacity to remain faithful to one's marriage vow, resisting all temptations to adultery and desertion;

— marriage is a 'sacrament', enabling husband and wife to love one another as Christ loves the Church; Christians are called to an ideal of constant fidelity and perfect love.

St Thomas Aquinas

BBC Hulton Picture Library

Church's Attitudes towards Divorce and Remarriage

From the very beginning, the binding force of Jesus' words was constantly in the mind of the Fathers of the Church. The ideal of the indissolubility of marriage was always recognised. Nevertheless, the question was asked: what can be done for Christians who have experienced divorce and wish to remarry? History tells us that, within the East to this day, and within the West for more than a thousand years, there was only one answer: to exercise tolerance and leniency and not to condemn.

■ Practice within the West: increasing strictness

Since Roman law permitted any divorced person to remarry, the only thing that would have prevented Christians from remarrying was clear teaching on the subject in the Bible. Such teaching, however, was regarded as ambiguous because, while clear about an adulterous wife not remarrying, it wasn't at all clear about a husband in the same situation. As a result, many bishops recognised infidelity as grounds for divorce, and some allowed husbands, but not wives, to remarry.

St Ambrose was the first to write that no marriage should be dissolved for any reason: *'What God has joined together, let no man put asunder'* — and this applies to men as well as women! St Augustine, as we have seen, followed his teacher in emphasising the indissolubility of the marriage bond, a sacrament of the faithfulness of Christ to his Church.

A few centuries would pass, however, before the Western Church would accept this teaching. It was only in the twelfth century that Pope Alexander III decided that mutual consent was the basis of a valid marriage and that, of itself, it was an unbreakable contract. Since then, the Church has always held that a properly celebrated and consummated marriage cannot be dissolved. The Council of Trent, in 1563, defined the indissolubility of such marriages, but in doing so, did not wish to condemn the practice of the Eastern Church. To this we now turn.

■ Practice within the East: principle of economy

Practice within the Eastern Orthodox tradition has developed quite differently and can be described simply:

▲ it upholds, in its teaching and pastoral care, the ideal of indissolubility: Christian marriage symbolises the love and respect that married people should always have for each other 'in the Lord';

▲ it considers divorce as tragic and a consequence of human sinfulness;

▲ out of pastoral concern, and remembering the Lord's words on forgiveness, the Eastern Church offers victims of divorce the opportunity for repentance and a fresh beginning. This second marriage is regarded as a real marriage, but not a sacramental marriage;

▲ it is, fundamentally, an application of the sacraments in a merciful way.

The Vision of Marriage

Life-giving for Husband and Wife

In the documents of the Second Vatican Council, the heart of marriage is described in the following terms: 'an intimate partnership'; 'a communion of life and love'; 'the mutual gift of two persons'; 'a conjugal covenant'. It is described best in a beautiful passage from *Gaudium et Spes*:

'A man and a woman, who by the marriage covenant of conjugal love "are no longer two, but one flesh", render mutual help and service to each other through an intimate union of their persons and actions. Through this union, they experience the meaning of their oneness and attain it with growing perfection day by day. As a mutual gift of two persons, this intimate union, as well as the good of the children, imposes total fidelity on the spouses and argues for an un-breakable oneness between them...just as Jesus loved the Church and handed himself over on her behalf, the spouses may love each other with perpetual fidelity through mutual self-giving.'

(no.48)

Marriage, therefore, must first of all be life-giving for husband and wife, whereby they make each other more fully human, more fully alive. It is in this life-giving relationship that the image of God is to be found, in becoming one flesh. The husband is called to live for the wife, the wife for the husband. If such love is to grow and develop, ensuring faithfulness and trust no matter what the difficulties or upheavals may be, it demands important qualities:

— it demands a great act of faith: 'for better, for worse; for richer, for poorer; in sickness and in health'; such faithfulness must be acknowledged as a gift, only sustained by the faithfulness of God;

— such faithfulness demands constant communication, arising out of a profound reverence and respect for one another; above all, it requires listening to one another, with love, with our eyes as well as our ears, with full attention, and with understanding. Listening is one of the greatest services we can do for one another;

— such love must have a great capacity for healing and forgiveness; not sex, but the ability to forgive one another is required premarital experience. In the words of St Paul: 'Bear with one another; forgive each other as soon as a quarrel begins. The Lord has forgiven you; now you must do the same.' (Colossians 3:13ff);

— married love is expressed most eloquently in the language of human sexuality. It can express joy and thanksgiving, hope and reconciliation; it can communicate strength and the need for strengthening, comfort and the need for comforting; it can be solemn or just playful and casual. It is a most powerful means whereby a couple grow in their knowledge and love of one another. It is in such moments of love that Jesus communicates the nature of his own passionate love in a special way.

© Carlos Reyes

Life-giving in bringing to birth New Life

The Second Vatican Council describes the meaning of children in marriage in the following terms:

> *'Marriage and married love are by nature ordered to the procreation and education of children. Indeed children are the supreme gift of marriage and greatly contribute to the good of parents themselves.'*
>
> (Gaudium et Spes, no.50)

Married love, therefore, entails *procreation*: the creation of the new life of another person, made in the image and likeness of God; it is one of the most privileged ways husband and wife become, in some small way, imitators of God in his creative activity. It is for this reason that every baby must be a wanted baby, not necessarily a planned baby, but a wanted baby. Secondly, married love entails the *education* of children: bringing children alive as human beings, fostering their emotional growth, providing bonds of security and care, developing their talents, bringing out their full potential as people who are able to love.

Married couples should have a responsible attitude to the size of their families within the context of a desire to live a full Christian marriage. In the midst of uncertainty, married couples need help in coming to a genuinely responsible decision in this important area of concern. Perhaps the following considerations need to be taken into account:

- Does our decision arise out of a respect for life or not?

- Does our decision arise out of our love and respect for each other?

- Do we have genuine reasons for not having children at this time?

- Are we able to provide the proper formation and education necessary for the children that we already have?

In this context, we need to be sensitive when speaking of marriage as a vocation to parenthood. There are many couples who are infertile because of some biological inability to have children. It is estimated that such couples represent as much as 10 per cent of all marriages. For some, their desire for children is so strong that they are willing to undergo all manner of tests and treatment to have a child of their own. They experience, in some cases, a lot of heartache and need careful counselling to help them recognise the fruitfulness of their marriage. In addition to the possibility of adopting or fostering children, they must be helped to find other creative ways of sharing the love they bear for one another.

© Paul Wigginton

The Celebration of Marriage

Preparation for Marriage from Early Childhood

■ In the Home

When a mother or father holds a new-born baby, in the closeness, warmth and trust of that embrace, the child's preparation for marriage begins. It is in the first years of life that the foundations are laid for the way each of us is able to relate to others. Parents have the main responsibility for providing the atmosphere of love and openness in which hurts can be healed and problems overcome. The need for openness becomes more acute in adolescent years, but throughout a child's development, the example of parents and other adults has more influence than words. The child who grows up in a family where love and affection are freely given has a strong foundation for building adult relationships which have the marks of faithfulness and self-giving.

■ In the School

Schools can help by teaching children, in religion and science classes, about themselves, their bodies and their responsibilities towards others. But schools also have a profound effect through the way children are treated. If a school's pastoral care and discipline systems are based on respect for each child, the children will be more likely to develop the ability to form good relationships. Liturgies, drama, sport and social activities can all help children to grow in this way, if these activities are aimed at the personal development of each child. The more parents are consulted and involved by the school, the more effective the partnership will be.

■ In the Parish

Parishes can support parents in many ways as they struggle to give their children the love and example they need. The liturgy should reflect their needs and concerns, and welcome their involvement. Parish groups can give practical help to families with particular difficulties. Parish programmes for baptism, first communion and confirmation provide opportunities for parents to share their experiences and difficulties, as well as promoting closer co-operation between parish, home and school. Youth groups and associations can help young people to discover their values and their vocation in life, and parish communities can invite and appreciate the contribution of young people to their life and work.

Preparation in the Months before the Wedding

■ The Style of Preparation and its Importance

Couples wanting to marry in the Catholic Church are encouraged to give at least six months' notice to the parish clergy. This is not just to avoid disappointment over bookings but to ensure that couples are given as much help as possible in preparing for their marriage. The priest is responsible for making sure that each partner is free to marry, and that each understands what Christian marriage is and what it demands. He will fill in the necessary forms and arrange the details of the wedding service.

That is the minimum, but in many parishes much more help is available. Teams of ordinary married people, trained and supported by diocesan Marriage and Family workers and by organisations like the Catholic Marriage Advisory Council, offer courses for couples approaching marriage. Sometimes these are all-day meetings, or residential weekends like those offered by the Engaged Encounter movement, but most frequently they will be a series of four to six evening sessions. They are not lectures or classes, but guided discussions in a friendly and welcoming atmosphere, with plenty of time for each couple to get to know each other better and to make friends with other engaged couples as well as with people leading the course. The topics and approaches vary, but most courses would discuss questions like communication, the important values in life, what you expect from marriage, sexuality, children, the wedding liturgy and the Church's vision of marriage as sacrament, as well as some practical issues like finance and who does what in the house. In view of the tremendous challenge of the marriage vocation today, such preparation is vitally important.

■ Special Considerations for 'Mixed Marriages'

This shorthand term refers to marriages between Catholics and members of another Church or none, which are now the majority of marriages taking place in Catholic Churches in England and Wales. A dispensation or permission is still required for such marriages:

— in the case of a Catholic marrying a baptised Christian of another denomination, it can usually be given by the parish priest;

— if a Catholic wishes to marry a non-Christian, the permission of the bishop is needed.

In each case, the concern is that the Catholic partner's own faith and happiness should be safeguarded and that the partner who is not a Catholic should understand the nature and duties of Christian marriage. The Catholic partner is required to promise to do all in his or her power to preserve his or her own faith and to ensure that any children of the marriage will be brought up as Catholics.

Despite these regulations, the Catholic Church does have a deep respect for the human and religious rights of non-Catholic partners in mixed marriages, and encourages particular care of such couples in our parishes. *The Association of Interchurch Families* has been formed to support and encourage couples who are committed members of two different traditions. John Paul II has spoken of such marriages in the most positive terms:

> **'You live in your marriage the hopes and difficulties of the path to Christian unity. Express that hope in prayer together, in the unity of love. Together invite the Holy Spirit of love into your hearts and into your homes. He will help you to grow in trust and understanding.'**
>
> *Pope John Paul II, York, 1982*

© Carlos Reyes

© Carlos Reyes

The Wedding Liturgy

■ Marrying in Church

Every family has its way of celebrating important events and, in the family of the Church, it is by gathering for a service in church. Couples who are making the great step of giving themselves to each other for life want their family and friends and their fellow parishioners to know about it and to join with them in celebrating their love for each other. Amidst all the traditional trappings of a wedding, the Church service, whether simple or grand, expresses the meaning of this great event. Before God and the community of the Church, husband and wife pledge their love for each other, which is the image and sign of the love of God. Such love is not a secret and furtive thing; it is a love which is lived openly within the Christian community, proclaiming the possibilities of faithfulness and forgiveness.

■ Nuptial Mass or Wedding Service?

Because the Eucharist is at the centre of the Catholic faith, many couples choose to celebrate their marriage with a Nuptial Mass. Other couples, particularly where a difference of religious practice between the families could cause disunity at the time of communion, choose the Wedding Service without Nuptial Mass. Sometimes people have the impression that a Nuptial Mass takes much longer than a Wedding Service. In fact, the length of readings, the number of hymns and the delays for photographs are the most significant factors in how long a service will take.

■ Elements of the Rite

Within the Rite, there is a wide variety of scripture readings, prayers and blessings, from which the couple, with their priest, may choose the ones which express their faith and their hopes for their married life. Hymns and other pieces of music are chosen to enhance the celebration, and the Bidding Prayers are composed to express the personal hopes and prayers of the couple on their wedding day. The family and friends of the bride and groom can be involved in reading the Scriptures and the Bidding Prayers and, in the case of a Nuptial Mass, in bringing up the gifts of bread and wine for the Eucharist. Sometimes, a booklet can be prepared, including the readings, prayers and hymns chosen for the service, with the names of the bride and groom inserted in the promises they make.

In all these ways, the couple themselves and their family and friends can make each celebration of a marriage personal and unique. The more effort they put into preparing the service, the more memorable and significant it will be for them.

■ 'Till death do us part'

The promises which the couple make to one another, calling on the community to witness them, are the central element of the Marriage Rite. A marriage is made by the consent of the bride and groom to give themselves totally to each other:

'to have and to hold, for better for worse, for richer for poorer, in sickness and in health, to love and to cherish, till death do us part.'

As the couple make these promises to each other, and call upon everyone present to witness them, they should do this *facing each other* and in full view of the congregation. The bride and groom are ministers of this sacrament for each other; the priest is simply the witness. The couple are also the main symbol of the sacrament. The ring or rings symbolise their love for each other, but they themselves are the clearest witness to that love, which is in turn the sign of God's love for his people.

■ Possible Future Developments

The present Rite of Marriage has been used since 1970 and is already in the process of being revised. We do not know yet what form the new Rite will take; the following are just a few suggestions which are beginning to emerge from a process of widespread consultation that is going on at the moment:

▲ The present Rite is the Universal Roman Rite and therefore is in need of considerable adaptation to accommodate local circumstances. It is possible that the new Rite will restore some of the richness of the traditional English and Welsh rites.

▲ More emphasis needs to be placed upon what belongs to the heart of the sacrament of marriage: the selfless love of Christ for his Church. This means reflecting more the biblical richness of God's love for his people. It has been said, with some justification, that an atheist could recite the present formula of consent without difficulty!

▲ Since the family represents the 'domestic Church', the new Rite must encourage more involvement on the part of the family and the community.

▲ Finally, the new Rite needs to emphasise more clearly the role of the bride and groom as ministers of the sacrament. Perhaps, in time, they will be the ones to welcome people to the service and lead the prayers and blessings. It must be more obvious that the priest is there only as a witness.

The Church's Pastoral Concern for Marriage and Family Life

The Church's Priority: Faithfulness in Marriage

The heart of every bride and every groom on their wedding day is filled with hopes and dreams for a life of happiness and love with their partner. For the majority of couples, many of these dreams will become realities and they will still be together in their old age. For such dreams to bear fruit, however, they need strong support from the parish community:

The Church must not waver in its concern to uphold the principle of indissolubility, flowing from the Gospel demand for life-long fidelity in marriage.

The quality of family life depends directly on the standard of life within the local community. The Church, therefore, must do all it can to ensure

proper housing conditions, the provision of employment, and the creative use of leisure time.

There must be concern to ensure adequate marriage preparation, as we have described it above; and also, there must be continuing support for marriage and family life in all its phases, with particular attention being given to the early years of marriage. Nearly fifty per cent of all marital breakdowns have taken place before the tenth wedding anniversary.

The parish community must support marriage and family life by prayer; by celebration of anniversaries; occasional renewal of marriage vows; the frequent mention of the concerns and needs of families in homilies and bidding prayers throughout the year.

The parish must, above all, be a welcoming community, where families feel at home and are encouraged to share their joys and hopes, their problems and difficulties. Groups like Marriage Encounter, Family and Social Action and the Grail Family Circles are all dedicated to supporting couples and families in their struggle to live out the values they hold dear. But, often, informal networks can provide this kind of mutual support.

The Church's Support when a Marriage fails

The Church has great admiration for those who bear witness to the indissoluble and irrevocable love of Christ by their faithfulness to their commitment, even when their married life is marred by pain and difficulty. That is why married couples must constantly be encouraged to strengthen and support their union and not allow it to die. Even when a relationship has fallen apart and separation occurs, every attempt must be made to bring it alive again; we must not conclude too quickly that a marriage is dead.

But for some, the failures and disappointments in their marriage will be too much to bear; the dreams become nightmares and all hope of happiness and love in their marriage is lost. Here, too, the Church has compassion for those married people whose pain and difficulty is so great that they must separate from their partners.

'We must reach out with love — the love of Christ — to those who know the pain of failure in marriage; to those who know the loneliness of bringing up a family on their own; to those whose family life is dominated by tragedy or by illness of mind or body. I praise all those who help people wounded by the breakdown of their marriage, by showing them Christ's compassion and counselling them according to Christ's truth.'

John Paul II, York, 1982

■ Legal Separation/Civil Divorce

Although the Church recognises that it may be necessary, from a legal and financial point of view, for a separated husband or wife to obtain a legal separation or civil divorce in order to protect their own rights and those of their children, this civil procedure has no effect on the marital status of the couple as far as the Church is concerned. Once a couple are validly married in the Catholic Church, no civil procedure can annul or invalidate their marriage. Nor does such a legal separation or civil divorce prevent a Catholic from receiving communion.

■ Nullity

If a person, whose marriage has broken down, feels that from the beginning of the marriage there was something so wrong or lacking in the relationship that it may not have been a valid marriage in the first place, that person has the right to ask the Diocesan or Regional Marriage Tribunals to investigate the validity of the marriage. This will involve a fairly lengthy process of collecting evidence from people who were close to the couple at the time of the marriage.

If the Tribunal finds that there was some serious impediment to the validity of the marriage, (such as one of the parties not being free to marry at the time, lacking the necessary judgement to commit themselves to marriage, or being unable to assume the responsibilities of marriage), a decree of nullity will be granted. This means that the marriage is judged never to have been a valid marriage, and so, each of the partners is free to marry someone else.

■ Remarriage

Many people who have suffered the breakdown of their marriage decide to enter into a second marriage. If they are Catholics, and have not obtained a decree of nullity with regard to their first marriage, this places them in apparent contradiction to the Church's firm belief in the permanence or indissolubility of marriage. Usually, this means that, although they are welcome at the celebration of the Eucharist, and should be given every other help in their struggle to live in faithfulness to the Gospel, they may not receive the sacraments.

Despite the difficulties over reception of the sacraments, the Church has been quite clear in expressing its concern and support for any of its members who are separated or divorced. Groups like the *Association of Separated and Divorced Catholics* have the backing of the bishops, both nationally and locally.

Nevertheless, being denied the sacraments is a cause of great pain and hardship to many people who feel deprived of the grace and help they still need, and it causes much heart-searching and debate amongst bishops, priests, moral theologians, and ordinary Catholics. In 1980 delegates to the National Pastoral Congress voted overwhelmingly in favour of Catholics in second marriages receiving the Eucharist and, later in that same year, the Synod *On the Role of the*

Family urged a closer study of the practice of the Eastern Churches which we described earlier. In this deeply sensitive area the Church's responsibility is twofold:

▲ She has a duty to married people and to the world not to weaken her proclamation of God's plan that marriage is for life;

▲ and yet, her basic instinct must be to reflect the attitude of Jesus in the Gospels who showed such compassion to those who had experienced failure in life and now desired to share his company.

Further Reading

Coventry, John. *Mixed Marriages Between Christians*, Catholic Truth Society, 1978
Dominian, Jack. *Marital Breakdown*, Penguin, 1968
Dominian, Jack. *Marriage, Faith and Love*, Darton, Longman & Todd, 1981
Dominian, Jack. *An Outline of Contemporary Christian Marriage*, Liverpool Institute of Socio-Religious Studies, 1976
Green, Wendy. *The Future of the Family*, Mowbray, 1984
Haughton, Rosemary. *The Theology of Marriage*, Clergy Book Service, 1971
Kasper, Walter. *Theology of Christian Marriage*, Burns & Oates, 1980
Sands, Ernest. *Marriage Preparation and Celebration*, Unitape, 1982 [audiotape]
Thomas, David M. *Christian Marriage*, Michael Glazier, 1983
Twomey, Gerald S. *When Catholics Marry Again*, Winston Press, 1982

PRIESTHOOD

Changing Role of the Priest

Many Catholics still remember the days when there was no ambiguity about the role of the priest within our parishes:

▲ we experienced the Church principally as an hierarchical Church with a strong emphasis on the experience of authority from the top; you would never argue with Father!

▲ the priest, therefore, would automatically be regarded as the one who had sole responsibility for affairs within the parish; he would speak quite naturally of 'My Parish';

▲ the priest's position within the parish was well reflected upon the altar as he celebrated Mass; he alone was the celebrant and only he could touch the sacred elements; the Mass was generally regarded as something 'done' by the priest and 'watched' by the people; again, it would be natural for him to speak of 'My Mass';

▲ in times of trouble and anxiety, people would automatically turn to the priest for help: in times of sickness, in times of marriage and family difficulties; if advice was needed on a whole range of issues;

▲ the priest's position was symbolised in his quite distinctive life-style: he would always be addressed as 'Father'; he would be immediately recognisable in his distinctive clerical dress and was evidently a 'man set apart' because of his commitment to a celibate way of life.

Priests, therefore, were special people who represented God, who represented the Church — in fact *were* the Church — who taught in the name of God and distributed the sacraments. But times are changing and the process of adjustment required both by priests and people has not been easy.

First of all, developments within society have meant that the priest is no longer the person everyone turns to for help. Marriage Guidance Councils, Child Guidance Clinics, social workers and psychiatrists have taken over many of the jobs the priest used to do. Furthermore, we live in a world in which authority is uniquely exposed to scrutiny and criticism. People have been encouraged to be critical and think for themselves. All of this has been made possible by the rapid expansion of education and the total volume of available knowledge. No longer can those in authority bank on the unquestioning trust of their subjects.

At the same time a new model of Church has emerged since Vatican II which has had a profound effect on the role of the priest:

▲ we are now encouraged to think of the Church as a 'Communion' in which priests and people are partners in the mission of Christ;

▲ priest and people together are called to share responsibility for the affairs of the parish; good leadership cannot be exercised nowadays without public discussion and shared planning for the future; we speak now of 'our parish';

▲ this shared responsibility is reflected in our celebration of the Eucharist, where a vital element of the priest's role is to foster participation, drawing together the many ministries of reader, cantor, lay minister of communion etc;

▲ far from being a man of God set apart, a priest is called to be a servant of the People of God, demanding a personal ministry close to the experience of people's lives.

In addition to the changes, fundamental questions are being asked about the future of the priesthood: Is there a place for married priests? will there soon be women priests? will there be a variation of part-time and full-time priests? All of these and more, we will need to bear in mind as we reflect on this sacrament of the ordained ministry.

Origins of the Priesthood in the New Testament

The Priesthood of Jesus Christ

The New Testament only knows one priesthood, the priesthood of Jesus Christ. This theme is reflected upon in the Letter to the Hebrews which highlights so many aspects which belong to the heart of the ministry of Jesus:

Jesus is one of us:

'For it is not as if we had a high priest who was incapable of feeling our weaknesses with us; but we have one who has been tempted in every way that we are, though he is without sin.'

(Hebrews 4:15)

What explains the impact of Jesus is nothing less than his sheer humanity; he presents himself as one who understands our weakness from personal experience.

Jesus is compassionate:

'He can sympathise with those who are ignorant or uncertain because he too lives in the limitations of weakness...'

(Hebrews 5:2)

Jesus was the friend of sinners and spoke to them with such sympathy it almost passes our understanding: Mary Magdalen, the publicans, the drop-outs. These people received nothing but kindness and compassion.

Jesus is faithful:

['Although he was Son, he learnt to obey through suffering...] let us not lose sight of Jesus, who leads us in faith and brings it to perfection.'

(Hebrews 12:2)

The Gospels speak of the inner struggle of Jesus as he sought to do the will of the Father. Faithfulness to the will of the Father did not come easily: 'Father, let this cup pass me by'. And yet we know that Jesus enters into the experience of abandonment on the cross and loves to the end.

Jesus is a Priest for ever:

'...this one, because he remains for ever, can never lose his priesthood. It follows, then, that his power to save is utterly certain, since he is living for ever to intercede for all who come to God through him.'

(Hebrews 7:25)

We know that the darkness Jesus experienced on the cross was not the ultimate truth of his life. When all seemed lost, he extended forgiveness to those who nailed him to the cross and promised paradise to one who was crucified with him. In that same love all of us have access to God.

All share in the Priesthood of Jesus Christ

A fundamental truth of the New Testament is that through baptism all believers are commissioned to proclaim the Good News of Jesus Christ. In St Peter's first letter we read:

> **'You are a chosen race, a royal priesthood, a consecrated nation, a people set apart to sing the praises of God who called you out of darkness into his wonderful light.'**
>
> *1 Peter 2:9*

Appointing of the elders

The Spirit of Christ is within all of us as an inner illumination, opening our hearts to the Gospel. This means that all, without exception, have a responsibility for building up the body of Christ and sharing in its mission. Whether as prophet, teacher, healer, minister of hospitality and charity, catechist or exorcist, the task of building up the body of Christ is addressed to, and accepted by, all Christians. All, whatever their specific calling, must reflect those essential gifts of the Spirit: love, joy, peace, patience, kindness, goodness, trustfulness, gentleness and self-control *(Galatians 5:22)*. Within the body of Christ, there are no honorary members!

The Need for Leadership

It was natural that the apostles should assume this role in the beginning. They had been with the Lord throughout his public ministry and were privileged witnesses of the resurrection. From early on, Peter was accepted as their spokesman *(Acts 2:14)* and all were listened to and respected. Their essential task was to be a leader in prayer, a preacher of the Gospel and a source of unity in times of dissension.

As the work of the Church developed, there was evident need of additional forms of leadership to help in the work of instructing, baptising, healing and encouraging the people who sought to know the Lord. And so, Paul and Barnabas, for example, 'appointed elders' *(Acts 14:23)* in each community to watch over the faith of the people. In other areas, 'espiscopos' or overseer became the term to describe the person with responsibility for the growing local Church. Deacons, too, were appointed as assistants to these leaders, Stephen *(Acts 6:8-10)* and Philip *(Acts 8:4-13)* being the most well known.

According to Paul's letter to Titus the criteria for appointing elders was that they be men of irreproachable character with the support of a good marriage and well-behaved children; they must be men of hospitality and must have a 'firm grasp of the unchanging message of the tradition' *(Titus 1:8-9)*. Above all, they must remember the attitude of Jesus when he spoke about leadership. They must not lord it over people in their care:

'No: anyone who wants to be
great among you must be your servant,
and anyone who wants to be first among you
must be slave to all.
For the Son of Man himself did not come
to be served but to serve,
and to give his life as a ransom for many.'
Mark 10:42-45

The parable of what Jesus was, what he expressed, and what he urged his disciples to emulate, is in the action of washing their feet, the most menial task of all:

'...he then poured water into a basin and began to wash the disciples' feet and to wipe them with the towel he was wearing. He came to Simon Peter, who said to him, "Lord, are you going to wash my feet?" Jesus answered, "At the moment you do not know what I am doing, but later you will understand." "Never!" said Peter "You shall never wash my feet." Jesus replied, "If I do not wash you, you can have nothing in common with me."... "If I then, the Lord and Master, have washed your feet, you should wash each other's feet. I have given you an example so that you may copy what I have done to you."'

(John 13:5-15)

Important Stages of Development

First Three Centuries: the Rise of the Local Bishop

As the first generation of witnesses and apostles disappeared, the role of elders and presbyters grew in importance as they assumed leadership within the local communities and were entrusted with the task of preserving the tradition. In some places the presiding elder alone was called 'episcopos' or 'bishop' because he held overall responsibility for affairs in the local Church and would naturally preside at the celebration of the Eucharist. And so, for example, in 110, St Ignatius could write:

> 'No one should do anything that pertains to the Church without the bishop's permission. The only proper Eucharist is one which is celebrated by the bishop or one of his representatives.'
>
> (Letter to the Smyrnaeans, 8)

Development during this period was naturally a gradual one because in many places, such as Rome for example, a form of group leadership prevailed. However, in the midst of so much variation, there was increasing concern for unity both in doctrine and practice. This was regarded essentially as the task of the bishops, who began to view themselves as 'successors of the apostles' in matters of faith. No one spoke with greater emphasis than St Cyprian of Carthage (d.258):

> 'You must realise that the bishop is where the Church is and the Church is where the bishop is, and that whoever is not with the bishop, is not in the Church.'
>
> (Letters 66,8)

Throughout this period the basic pattern of ministry within the Church would be as follows:

lay people continued to exercise many ministries according to their particular gifts; they played an important role in Synods and Councils and helped to choose the bishop;

deacons were full-time assistants to the bishops, especially in liturgical and financial matters; after the bishop they were the most influential group within the Church;

presbyters did not yet exercise a full-time ministry; they shared in the bishop's weekly Eucharist and acted as a kind of parish council in the various towns and cities;

the *bishop* was increasingly the leader of the local Church and his main tasks were to preach the Gospel, preside at the Eucharist, and to maintain unity with the faith of the apostles. In the rite of ordination, hands were imposed upon him by other bishops while everyone prayed that the Spirit might come upon them to enable them to become rulers and shepherds of their people.

The model of Church during this time was still that of a 'Communion' in which everyone was encouraged to take an active part in the spread of the Gospel. But the pattern soon began to change and we need to ask ourselves:

- How did the roles of bishop and presbyter change so radically?
- How did the clergy assume so much authority?
- Why did the laity become spectators at their own act of worship?

Gradual Breakdown of Church as 'Communion'

■ Presbyters come into their own

When Christianity became the official religion of the Roman Empire, the bishops not only assumed responsibility for a number of churches but inevitably became more involved in matters of State. Clearly a choice had to be made. The choice was principally for the latter and this is where the presbyters came into their own. Whilst remaining under the bishops' direction, they frequently presided at eucharistic and baptismal liturgies where the bishop could not be present.

About this time, prominent Christians like St Jerome and St John Chrysostom tended to speak of presbyters in exalted terms and so the question naturally arose: what is the difference between a bishop and a presbyter? They argued that bishops and presbyters were basically equal because there was no greater power than that of being able to celebrate the Eucharist. The only 'extra' that a bishop had was in the realm of jurisdiction which meant that he exercised greater authority in the Church. This whole debate had a number of consequences for the future development of ministry within the Church:

- the bishop's task was seen primarily as one of administration;
- the presbyter became the pastoral leader of the local Church;
- the diaconate as a separate ministry disappeared altogether.

■ The Beginnings of Clerical Privilege

With the growing influence of the Church within society, bishops and priests began to enjoy a status similar to their political counterparts: they were referred to as officials; they were exempted from military service; and they did not have to pay taxes. By the end of the fifth century, both bishops and clergy were wearing a long robe as a sign of their status within society. This marked the beginning of clerical dress which has lasted to our own day. By now, the distinction between 'clergy' and 'laity' was firmly established.

■ 'Priesthood' versus 'Ministry'

Bishops and priests were described more and more in terms borrowed from the Jewish priesthood of the Old Testament. Like their Jewish counterparts, therefore, they would be seen primarily as performers of sacred rites, as having special access to God and making intercession on behalf of the people. In this context, the priesthood was increasingly understood as a liturgical function and less and less as a ministry of service within the Christian community. This had a number of profound effects on the shape of liturgy within the Church:

▲ the action of the Mass belonged entirely to the priest while the people were passive spectators;

▲ private Masses became commonplace and many priests were ordained just to cope with the number required: hence the term 'massing-priests';

▲ the priesthood was now defined exclusively as a power to consecrate the bread and wine into the body and blood of Christ.

■ Implications of the Rite of Ordination

The sacrament of ordination made bishops and priests members of a distinct 'order' within the Church, a rite which consisted essentially in the laying-on of hands. During the early Middle Ages, however, this rite underwent a few significant changes:

▲ bishops, priests and deacons received the vestments they would wear during liturgical celebrations;

▲ symbolic tokens of their responsibilities were handed over: deacons were given the book of the Gospels; priests, a chalice and paten;

▲ ordination conferred a power: in the case of priests, the power to consecrate and offer the Eucharist.

This sacrament came to be regarded as the only effective source of ministry within the Church. Such ministries that existed amongst the laity were essentially steps on the way to the priesthood. All other ministries and positions of leadership shared by the laity in earlier times were now absorbed into the priesthood. Priests alone were the human instruments through which God acted and bestowed blessings upon his people.

Such was the basic understanding of priesthood which has lasted right down to our own times. It has shaped our patterns of training for the priesthood in seminaries, set apart, away from the world; it is responsible for the parish priest we have known and loved who spoke quite naturally of 'My Parish' and 'My Mass'. But what has happened in the meantime to that baptismal calling which belongs to all within the People of God? The answer was to emerge with Vatican II.

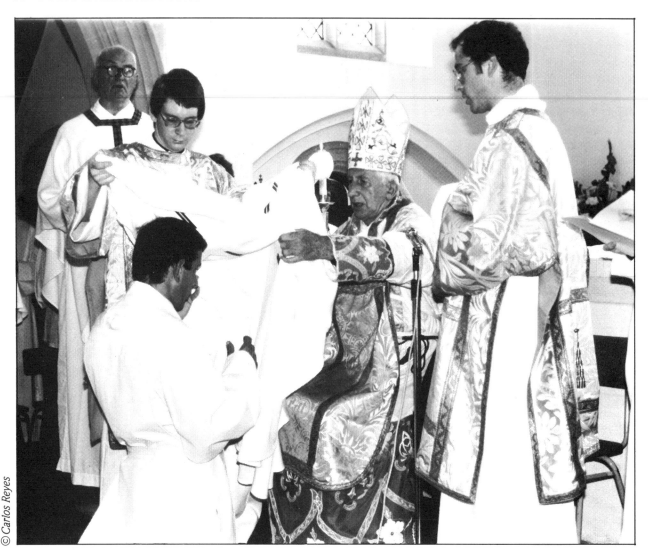

© Carlos Reyes

The Ordained Ministry: A Call to Serve

One People of God

A basic insight of Vatican II is that a starting-point for any consideration of the meaning of ordination is that there is just one People of God *(Lumen Gentium, 9)*. It points out that faith and baptism are the primary sources of *all* ministry within the Church — which means that there are no second-class citizens within the fellowship of Christians. All have equal rights and obligations, even though their capacities, desires or abilities to exercise them may differ widely. There are people who are leaders in prayer, others with compassion and time for the sick, people who take responsibility for those in need. We are only just beginning to realise the many gifts that are available in the Church and that have not been tapped. No one person, no matter how talented or well trained, can possibly lay claim to all the gifts or be solely responsible for any new initiative. We have yet to benefit from many new forms of ministry and service, especially from women who for too long have been excluded from so many effective forms of ministry.

It is only within this context that the ordained ministry has any meaning. The essential task of this ministry is to enable the many varied gifts of the Spirit to flourish within the community and so build up the body of Christ. In particular, Jesus calls such leadership to give special attention to the poor and the needy with whom he identified himself and to whom he showed nothing but kindness and compassion. A striking example of such leadership is given to us in the person of Archbishop Romero who became one with the sufferings of the people of El Salvador:

> 'Every time we come closer to the poor, we discover the true face of the suffering servant of God. There we come closer to knowing the mystery of Christ who becomes human and poor through us...we want a Church that is shoulder to shoulder with the poor people of El Salvador.'

This is a powerful image of committed priesthood and reveals the inner meaning of that gift which Christ has given to the whole Church. It must be a gift which is motivated by a great love for the people and a strong commitment to the task of helping people to realise their true calling as bearers of Christ for one another.

Meaning of the Ordained Ministry Today

■ The Role of the Bishop

Vatican II had a great deal to say about bishops. First of all, it declared that 'by episcopal consecration is conferred the fullness of the sacrament of orders', thereby making a bishop a member of the College of Bishops, sharing responsibility for the world-wide mission of the Church. And so a major part of a bishop's task is to take part in meetings both internationally and nationally which demand listening to, reflecting and responding to the experiences of the whole body of believers. Examples would be the Second Vatican Council itself and subsequent Synodal Meetings in Rome, such as the one taking place in the Autumn of 1987 on the subject of the Laity. This consciousness of belonging to the universal Church is vital, if local Churches, and individuals too, are not to live a monadic existence, private and autonomous, but are to live in communion with one another, encouraging and challenging each other in love and with mutual concern for true peace and justice. Our bishops, therefore, have encouraged links between English dioceses and dioceses in the Third World, such as the connection with Peru in the Liverpool Archdiocese (LAMP).

Within this shared responsibility for the universal Church, the bishop has a particular responsibility within the local Church of 'sanctifying, teaching, and governing in the name of Christ'. Consciousness of belonging to the local Church is best experienced when the bishop celebrates the Eucharist with his priests and people, especially in the Cathedral on Holy Thursday, but also on his frequent visitations around the parishes during the year. In the words of Vatican II: 'He is the visible principle and foundation of unity in his particular Church'. This must find expression in many other ways:

— a bishop needs to be one who is visibly a man of prayer: 'bishops should aim to make of one mind in prayer all who are entrusted to their care...';

— a bishop needs to establish a close relationship with his fellow-priests: 'He should regard (his priests) as his sons and friends. He should always be ready to listen to them and cultivate an atmosphere of easy familiarity with them...';

— amongst his many responsibilities, a bishop's special task is to proclaim the Gospel and be the guardian of faithful witness within the local community, enabling healing and reconciliation to take place wherever it is needed.

All these are amongst the many concerns of a bishop but they do not lie with him alone; he must share his responsibilities with his fellow-bishops, priests and people. As the bishops were made aware at the National Pastoral Congress, held in Liverpool in 1980, it is only in the midst of their people that bishops can truly understand what it is to be a bishop in the Church of today.

© Carlos Reyes

© Carlos Reyes

■ The Role of the Priest

Despite the many responsibilities a bishop has within his diocese, he is still a far-away figure to most of his people. In practice, it is the priest within the parish who does most of the preaching and the administering of the sacraments. As co-worker with the bishop, the priest is called upon to be a powerful symbol of the care and compassion of Christ, a minister of Christ's healing and reconciliation. No longer is he to be looked on simply as a performer of sacred rites, but as one who co-ordinates the many ministries which are available in parishes today and enables the 'saints' to use their gifts for the service of God amongst his people.

This means, first of all, that a priest must be a man of God, his close friend (John Paul II, Heaton Park, 1982). Like the bishop, the priest, too, must be visibly a man of prayer, sharing privacy with the Lord that he might share himself more fully with his people. In the words of John Wesley: 'I have so much to do that I must spend several hours in prayer before I am able to do it'! But a priest must not simply pray alone; he must share his moments of prayer with his fellow-priests upon whom he depends for mutual support; with the people of his parish, encouraging a mutual sharing of hopes and joys, sorrows and frustrations; and especially with the sick, not just praying *for* them but *with* them.

A challenging responsibility of the priest is to be a minister of the Word. A priest is asked to make his own those words of St John Chrysostom: 'My priesthood is to preach and announce the Gospel'. It is challenging because so much has happened both within the Church and within society in recent years that it is not easy to preach the Gospel with confidence. Necessary time must be given for preparation

© Carlos Reyes

and study; a priest's personal life-style must be one of openness and friendliness; he must know the people entrusted to his care and, for this, there is no substitute for visiting people in their homes. A priest must take to heart those words of St Augustine: 'Allow me to listen to you so that I can then talk to you'.

Celebration of the Eucharist has always been at the heart of a priest's ministry, and its worthy celebration must always be a first priority (John Paul II, Cardiff, 1982). A priest's role is to be leader, fostering participation, drawing together the many ministries, raising the spirits of the congregation. This can best be done fruitfully if the priest understands the flow of the liturgy and its various parts, but, above all, the importance of silence, providing an opportunity for the Spirit to speak directly into the hearts of the people gathered for worship.

The shape of the Eucharist today reflects the basic understanding of the Church as a 'communion'. This means that the priest's ministry is essentially a shared ministry. Once again, in the words of John Paul II:

'Every priest relies on the faith and talents of his parish community...The partnership between priests and people is built upon prayer, collaboration and mutual respect and love.'
(Heaton Park, 1982)

Such mutual respect demands sharing in all aspects of parish life: knowledge about the finances of the parish, preparation of the liturgy, and involvement in the process of decision-making, all of which need the co-ordination of something like a parish council.

The role of the priest comes to a focus in the rite of ordination which is now most appropriately celebrated in the new priest's parish. The local Church is well represented as the bishop, in the company of many of the priests of the diocese, lays hands upon the new priest in silence. This moment is followed by the prayer of consecration:

'Almighty Father, grant to this servant of yours the dignity of the priesthood. Renew within him the spirit of holiness. As a co-worker with the order of bishops may he be faithful to the ministry that he receives from you, Lord God, and be to others a model of right conduct.'

■ The Role of the Deacon

The diaconate is now restored as a distinct order within the Church and is no longer considered simply as the last hurdle before the priesthood. It is open to married men who must ensure that they have the full support of their families. Candidates are normally from the parish in which they will be working. Their formation period lasts for three years and centres round a monthly study day and an annual residential retreat. As deacons, they will continue in their secular occupations to support their families.

The deacon's commitment is permanent and his ministry involves a specific teaching role: proclaiming the Gospel at Mass, preaching and preparing people for the sacraments. Other liturgical functions include assisting at Mass, administering Holy Communion, presiding at baptisms and funerals, and blessing marriages.

Many other responsibilities include caring for the sick and the poor of the community, and promoting the full integration of various groups into the life of the parish community.

Who Can be Ordained?

Married Men?

In the Western Church, the present law forbids married persons from being ordained; except in the few cases of convert clergymen, celibacy is a requirement for both priests and bishops. The association of the Christian ordained leaders with the Old Testament priesthood led the Church to request priests and bishops to abstain from sexual intercourse, as the Old Testament priests had done, for reason of ritual purity. The initial request for voluntary celibacy in the fourth century eventually led the Western Church to impose celibacy on both bishops and priests in 1139. The Catholic Church in the East has continued the tradition of married priests, although bishops are required to be celibate.

One of the essential aspects of being a minister of a community is to be free for one's people, which means being as available and as accessible as possible. For centuries, it has been the Church's understanding that the only way a priest can provide adequate service for his people is by being committed to a celibate way of life. This is not just a question of practicalities; the priest by his very way of life is dramatically symbolising the orientation of all things to the kingdom of God. Far from having a negative effect on human relationships, it should enrich the possibilities of giving and receiving in love and friendship, not only with fellow-priests, but especially with men and women, both married and single, within our parishes. If celibacy is to be truly a sign of the kingdom, then, it must find expression in flesh and blood and be supported by the whole community.

Because celibacy can only be a free gift of the Lord and not something forced upon someone as part of the total package deal of priesthood, there are increasing objections being made against compulsory celibacy. It is argued that, although Jesus was celibate, he did not require celibacy for his apostles and disciples. Furthermore, there are countless married priests of the Eastern rites, Protestant ministers, and rabbis, who are at least as available to their people as the average celibate priest. In fact, the experience of being married and being a parent can be an advantage in running a parish or even a diocese. It remains to be seen how the issues resolve themselves.

© Carlos Reyes

Women?

Unlike the celibacy question, the possibility of women becoming priests has traditionally been considered as being against the will of God. The arguments for this position are as follows:

- Jesus did not admit any women among the Twelve;

- Jesus did not even make an exception for Mary;

- only a male priest can truly represent Christ;

- for 19 centuries, no woman has received or-dination.

Today, however, when we are becoming increasingly conscious of the importance of the role of women within society, the traditional stance of the Church on this question is being challenged:

▲ The mere fact that Jesus did not do something does not mean that it cannot be done. It is true that Jesus did not choose any woman to be one of his apostles; but neither did he choose Romans or Greeks, only Jews. The principal reason for Jesus not choosing women would seem to be that in the circumstances of the time they would not be acceptable as spiritual leaders. They were the first to witness the resurrection and yet 'this story of theirs seemed pure nonsense' *(Luke 24:11)*!

▲ It is true that the priest is a sign of Christ; but isn't it true that within the body of Christ, both men and women are called to be a sign of Christ? We cannot present an understanding of the priest in a way which compromises that fundamental truth expressed so powerfully in the words of St Paul:

> **'All baptised in Christ, you have all clothed yourselves in Christ, and there are no more distinctions between Jew and Greek, slave and free, male and female, but all of you are one in Christ Jesus.'**
>
> *Galatians 3:27*

Again, only time will tell how this question will be resolved. Women are playing an increasing role within the Churches, and in a number of Churches, this includes the role of priesthood. We need to listen to these various voices; they call for old wrongs to be redressed and for new forms of ministry and service to be made possible. It may be that only the full partici-pation of women in the Church's ministry can really do justice to the compassion of Christ:

> *'How often have I longed to gather your children, as a hen gathers her brood under her wings, and you refused!'*
>
> (Luke 13:34)

Further Reading

Dalrymple, John. *Letting Go in Love*, Darton, Longman & Todd, 1986

Edwards, Paul. *The Theology of Priesthood*, Mercier Press, 1974

Power, David N. *Ministers of Christ and His Church*, Chapman, 1969

The Priesthood of the Ordained Ministry, Board of Mission for Unity, 1986

Ramsey, Michael. *The Christian Priest Today*, SPCK, 1969

Tillard, Jean. *What Priesthood Has the Ministry*, Grove Books, 1973